CHINA

BY RACQUEL FORAN

Essential Library
An Imprint of Abdo Publishing
abdobooks.com

ABDOBOOKS.COM
Published by Abdo Publishing, a division of ABDO, PO Box 398166, Minneapolis, Minnesota 55439.

Printed in the United States of America, North Mankato, Minnesota.
102022
012023

THIS BOOK CONTAINS RECYCLED MATERIALS

Cover Photos: Shutterstock Images (Great Wall of China, pattern)
Interior Photos: Shutterstock Images, 4–5, 8, 10, 12, 13, 14–15, 17, 21, 32, 52–53, 55, 60, 67, 80, 87, 88–89, 90; Peter Hermes Furian/Shutterstock Images, 18 (China); Web Tools/Shutterstock Images, 18 (globe); Sander Bos/Shutterstock Images, 20; Pav-Pro Photography Ltd./Shutterstock Images, 22; Karel Cerny/Shutterstock Images, 24–25; Dickson Lee/South China Morning Post/Getty Images, 26; Tristan Tan/Shutterstock Images, 27; Vadim Petrakov/Shutterstock Images, 30–31; Zhang Lang/China News Service/Getty Images, 34–35; Mark Brandon/Shutterstock Images, 36; Pictures From History/Universal Images Group/Getty Images, 37, 40; Zhu Wenzhe/Xinhua News Agency/Getty Images, 42; Everett Collection/Shutterstock Images, 44; DEA/Biblioteca Ambrosiana/De Agostini/Getty Images, 45; Bettmann/Getty Images, 48; Jeff Widener/AP Images, 50; AP Images, 51, 76; Servais Mont/Getty Images News/Getty Images, 56; Kevin Frayer/Getty Images News/Getty Images, 58; Paul Atkinson/Shutterstock Images, 59; Hafiz Johari/Shutterstock Images, 63; Ren Weihong/Imagine China/AP Images, 64; Vincent Thian/AP Images, 68–69; Shui Guotang/Imagine China/AP Images, 70; Selim Chtayti/Pool Agence France Presse/AP Images, 71; Kin Cheung/AP Images, 74; Shi Donghong/Imagine China/AP Images, 78–79; Ni Shaokang/Visual China Group/Getty Images, 83; Imagine China/AP Images, 91; Su Yang/Feature China/AP Images, 93; Ray Young/Feature China/AP Images, 95; Alexei Druzhinin/Sputnik/Kremlin Photo Pool/AP Images, 96–97; Artsem Vysotski/Shutterstock Images, 101

Editor: Layna Darling
Series Designer: Maggie Villaume

Library of Congress Control Number: 2022940309

PUBLISHER'S CATALOGING-IN-PUBLICATION DATA
Names: Foran, Racquel, author.
Title: China / by Racquel Foran
Description: Minneapolis, Minnesota: Abdo Publishing, 2023 | Series: Essential Library of Countries | Includes online resources and index.
Identifiers: ISBN 9781532199387 (lib. bdg.) | ISBN 9781098274580 (ebook)
Subjects: LCSH: China--Juvenile literature. | Asia--Juvenile literature. | China--History--Juvenile literature. | Geography--Juvenile literature.
Classification: DDC 951--dc23

CONTENTS

CHAPTER **ONE**

A TOUR OF CHINA

The 13-hour flight to Beijing from California was nearing its end. Betty looked out the airplane window. She hoped she could see the Great Wall of China from the plane. Betty and her high school classmates had been planning this cultural exchange trip to China for two years.

As the plane dipped below the cloud line, Betty could see land. First, the Da Hinggan and Xiao Hinggan mountain ranges came into sight. Soon the mountains disappeared, and Beijing sprawled out below her. A maze of densely packed buildings spread out for miles in every direction and stretched into a patchwork of fields.

The construction of the ultramodern Beijing Daxing International Airport was an enormous undertaking. The airport, one example of China's many infrastructure investments, opened in late 2019.

Before she knew it, the plane descended toward Beijing Daxing International Airport. Surrounded by a labyrinth of taxiing lanes and runways, the star-shaped terminal looked like something from a science fiction movie. Betty discovered the airport was huge but well designed, so it was easy to get from one end to the other.

The drive from the airport to central Beijing lasted about an hour. Vast fields and green spaces marked the geography surrounding the highway, with what looked like densely populated small neighborhoods dropped in the middle of them. But as the car got closer to the city, the fields became fewer, and the number of buildings increased. The urban landscape stretched as far as the eye could see.

BEIJING DAXING INTERNATIONAL AIRPORT

The Beijing Daxing International Airport opened in September 2019. It covers more than 18 square miles (46 sq km) including runways, annexes, and the terminal. At 7.5 million square feet (696,773 sq m), the terminal is the world's largest. It cost $11 billion to build. The star-shaped design ensures travelers never have to walk more than 1,970 feet (600 m) from the center of the building to the farthest gate. The Chinese government estimates that the airport will service 100 million passengers a year by 2040.[1]

DISCOVERING HIDDEN *HUTONGS*

When the minibus rolled to a stop and the chaperone said they had reached their destination, Betty was confused. They had stopped in an alley. She looked out the bus window and wondered where the hotel was; all she could see was an opening between the buildings. Then she saw a small sign that read "hotel." Betty followed her group through the opening. To her surprise, an entire neighborhood was tucked inside the gates.

They were staying in a converted *siheyuan* hotel in a *hutong*. First built by the Mongol Yuan dynasty between 1271 and 1368, hutongs are narrow streets and alleys lined by siheyuans. A siheyuan is a compound of buildings surrounding an open courtyard. Siheyuans are always asymmetrical. They can have more than one courtyard and a varying number of structures, but the main house or residence is always on the north-south axis, with smaller, less important buildings on the east and west sides. Hutongs form small villages within the larger city. Some families have lived in a single hutong for centuries.

With modernization and increased land values, many hutongs have disappeared. Visiting one that remains is a unique Chinese cultural experience. Every hutong gate is different. Some are so simple they are easy to miss. Others are adorned with stone lion heads and elaborate carvings. Betty's group's hutong was a surprise. The gate was nothing special, but the courtyard was a modern delight. Aside from the renovated siheyuan, there were coffee shops, bakeries, vegetable markets, hair salons, tourist shops, and several stalls selling local food and artisan items. There was a hidden world behind the walls of the alley.

THE FORBIDDEN CITY

On their first full day in Beijing, the group headed to the Forbidden City. The size of the compound was awe inspiring. A former imperial palace sitting in the heart of Beijing, it was the residence

Many of Beijing's hutongs have been demolished and redeveloped, but others have been protected and preserved.

of 24 emperors over a period of more than 500 years. It was called the Forbidden City because only imperial families and high officials could enter. There are 90 palace compounds within the property, including more than 900 buildings.[2] The last emperor's rule ended in 1924, and the imperial palace opened to the public the following year as the renamed Palace Museum. Named a United Nations Educational, Scientific and Cultural Organization (UNESCO) World Heritage site in 1987, it is home to the world's largest collection of ancient wooden structures.

Betty looked up as she entered the Wu Gate. All the palace rooftops were yellow, but each one looked different. Some were much larger than others. She would learn later that palaces with larger, double-eaved roofs were considered more important than palaces with smaller roofs.

Betty wished they had more than half a day at the Palace Museum, but she and her group were eager to visit Tiananmen Square. The Tiananmen gate separates Tiananmen Square from the Palace Museum. *Tiananmen* means "Gate of Heavenly Peace." The Monument to the People's Heroes and the Mao Zedong Memorial Hall are in Tiananmen Square. The Great Hall of the People, which was the group's next destination, is also in the square. Another building that is breathtaking in scale, the Great Hall is the home of the Chinese Communist Party (CCP), which controls China. Betty noticed that each of the flagstones in the 100-acre (40.5 ha) square was numbered.[3] Their guide explained this made it easier to coordinate parades

The Palace Museum spans 178 acres (72 ha) and is surrounded by a moat that is 170 feet (52 m) wide.[4]

The many structures of the Forbidden City sit behind Tiananmen Square in Beijing.

and marches. The square's connection to government celebration and grandeur has made it a place for political protest in the past.

HIGH SPEED TO SHANGHAI

Betty's group arrived at the train station early on the third day of the trip. They were heading to Shanghai, an 819-mile (1,318 km) trip by high-speed train. The train would travel at up to 217 miles

THE INCIDENT AT TIANANMEN SQUARE

In the 1980s, tens of thousands of Chinese students protested in Tiananmen Square to demand political reforms, including freedom of the press, freedom of speech, and democracy. In mid-May 1989, when Soviet leader Mikhail Gorbachev visited the country, one million protesters demonstrated in the square. After this, the CCP declared martial law and stationed army troops around Beijing. However, protesters blocked them from entering Tiananmen Square. On June 4, 1989, the government sent in tanks, and troops opened fire on anyone who blocked the path. The troops had emptied the square by the next day. The Chinese government said 241 people were killed and more than 7,000 injured.[6] Outside estimates of the toll were typically much higher.

per hour (350 kmh), getting them to Shanghai in about five hours. The Beijing South railway station was massive, bigger than many airports. The train itself was impressive too. Seventeen sleek white cars extended more than 1,440 feet (440 m) down the track.

They would pass through four provinces and 24 stations before arriving at their destination.[5] Betty settled into her seat and prepared to take in as much of the country as she could. The areas surrounding each station looked industrial. The train zoomed past fields, small communities, and large cities. Most of the buildings looked modern. Betty noticed that she could almost always see mountains in the distance.

When they arrived at the Shanghai Hongqiao railway station, they went straight to the Bund. Sometimes called the museum of buildings, the Bund is a promenade along the Huangpu River lined by a variety of architecturally significant and diverse structures. Betty noticed that every building looked very old, but they each were a

Streamlined high-speed trains whisk passengers between China's major metropolitan areas.

different architectural style. In stark contrast, across the river on the east side, the buildings in Pudong looked futuristic. Structures of all shapes, sizes, and heights rose from the riverbank, dominated the skyline, and reflected onto the river. Betty was curious about what other surprises China had to offer.

A LOOK AT CHINA

China is home to a civilization thousands of years old, but it also has some of the world's most modern cities. It has densely populated urban areas, but it also has vast regions that are uninhabited. Its long history has touched all aspects of today's world, from ancient medicine to modern high-tech consumer products. It exports more goods to more countries than any other nation.

China has a wealth of natural wonders. It is home to Earth's tallest mountain, highest plateau, third-largest freshwater source, third-largest river, and fifth-largest desert. It is also a country of human extremes. China is the world's most populous nation. It has the world's largest airport terminal and seven of the world's ten largest seaports. Its economy has grown dramatically since the 1980s, and the scope of its power and influence have made it a global leader.

China's incredible growth has improved standards of living for millions of the nation's citizens.

CHAPTER **TWO**

GEOGRAPHY

Encompassing most of eastern Asia, China's diverse geography includes all types of terrain. The landscape varies from dramatic mountains in the west to arid desert in the north, vast plains in the northeast, lush river valleys in the south, and densely populated deltas in the southeast.

Covering 3,705,407 square miles (9,596,960 sq km), China is slightly smaller than the United States, making it the fourth-largest country in the world.[1] It is surrounded by land on three sides, sharing borders with 14 different countries. Mongolia is to the north. It has China's longest shared border, at 2,877 miles (4,630 km).[2] Russia and North Korea lie to the northeast. Afghanistan, Kyrgyzstan, Tajikistan, Kazakhstan, and Pakistan form China's western border. India, Bhutan,

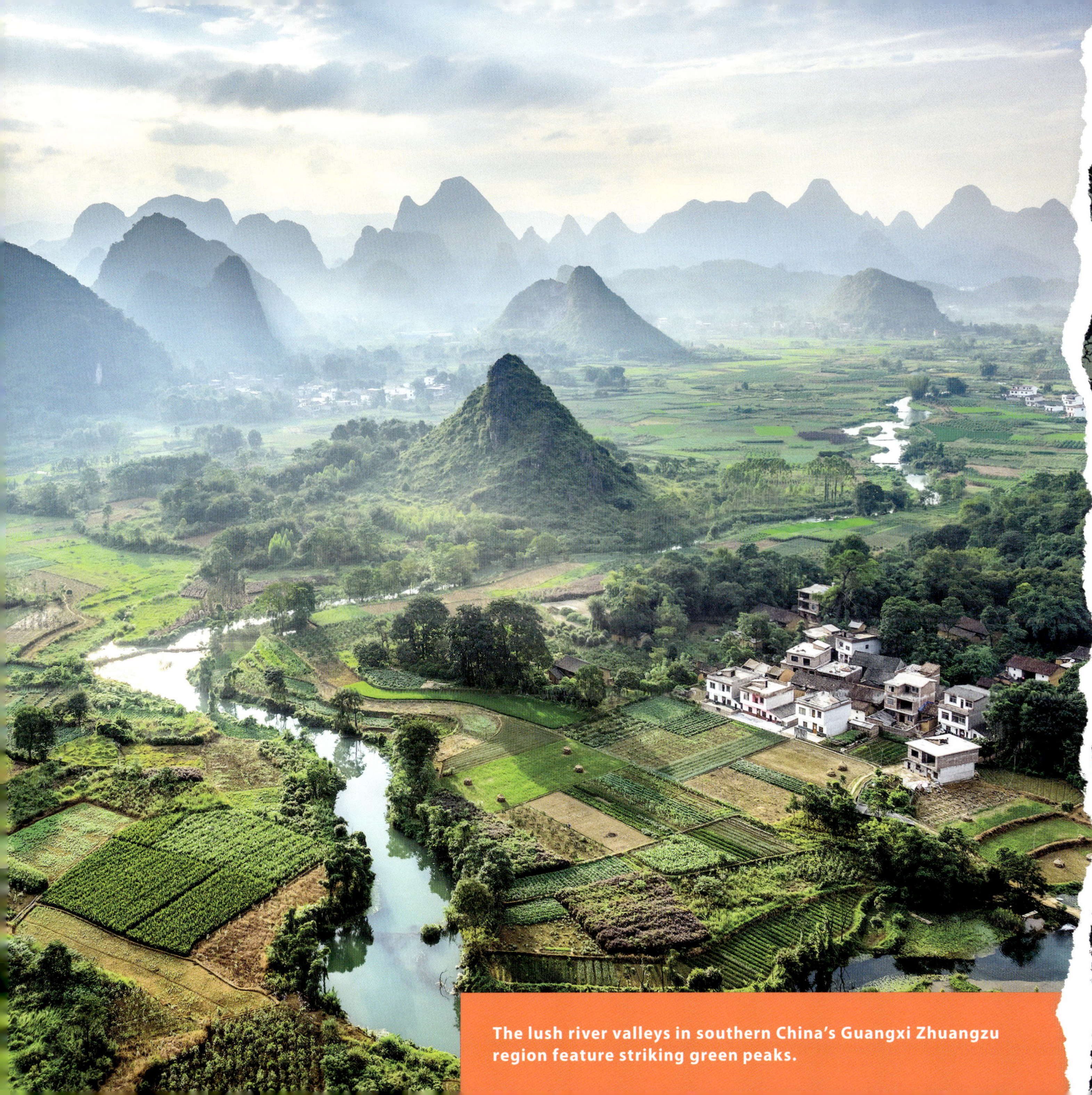

The lush river valleys in southern China's Guangxi Zhuangzu region feature striking green peaks.

Nepal, Burma, Laos, and Vietnam stretch across the southern border. The eastern border is formed by coastline, including the Yellow Sea, the East China Sea, and the South China Sea. Across these seas, China faces South Korea, Japan, and the Philippines.

China has more than 250,000 square miles (647,000 sq km) of wetlands, including river, marsh, and lake wetlands.[7]

MOUNTAINS AND RIVERS

The western and eastern regions of China differ greatly from each other. In the west, high mountain ranges dominate the landscape. China is home to Mount Everest, the world's highest mountain, which is in the Himalayas, the world's highest mountain range. The Tibetan Plateau, Earth's largest and highest plateau, is also in China. The plateau's average elevation is about 14,800 feet (4,500 m) above sea level. There are approximately 1,500 glacial lakes in the Tibetan Plateau.[3] China is also home to the longest mountain range in Asia. The Kunlun Mountains are about 1,250 miles (2,000 km) long and extend from the Gobi desert in northern China to the Tarim Pendi in Xinjiang, a region in western China.[4]

Rivers abound in China. More than 20,000 rivers cover an area of at least 38.6 square miles (100 sq km) each.[5] Thirty-six percent of China's rivers are interior, meaning they drain into inland lakes, are absorbed by salt marshes, or disappear into deserts.[6] Most rivers in the country begin in the Tibetan Plateau and drop dramatically in elevation from their source to their mouth. The two longest rivers, the Yangtze (Chang Jiang) and Huang He, as well as several others, flow east into the Pacific Ocean. In Tibet, the Yarlung Zangbo Jiang has carved the world's longest and deepest canyon on its way to draining into the Indian Ocean. The canyon is more than 300 miles (500 km) long and 17,000 feet (5,300 m) deep.[8] In western China, the Irtysh River flows north into the Arctic Ocean.

DESERTS, PLAINS, AND TERRACES

The Gobi desert, which straddles China and Mongolia, is the fifth-largest desert in the world. The tall Himalayan mountains block rain from reaching this landscape, leaving it arid. The amount of arid land is increasing steadily. The Gobi is the fastest-growing desert on the planet. An average of 2,250 square miles (5,827 sq km) of grassland per year has transformed into arid soil from a combination of human activity and

MOUNT EVEREST

In the Himalayas on the border between Nepal and China's Tibet region, Mount Everest rises 29,032 feet (8,849 m) above sea level. It presents difficult and hostile climbing conditions. The warmest it ever gets is –2 degrees Fahrenheit (–19°C), and weather can change suddenly, causing temperatures to drop and winds to whip up to 100 miles per hour (160 kmh). Edmund Hillary and his Sherpa guide Tenzing Norgay were the first people to reach the summit, accomplishing this on May 29, 1953. Since then, more than 7,500 people have made it to the summit. Almost 300 people have died attempting the climb.[9] The rugged terrain, lack of oxygen, and freezing weather make it difficult to retrieve the bodies of fallen climbers. Many of them remain on the mountain.

MAP OF CHINA

KEY:

- Capital
- City
- Point of Interest

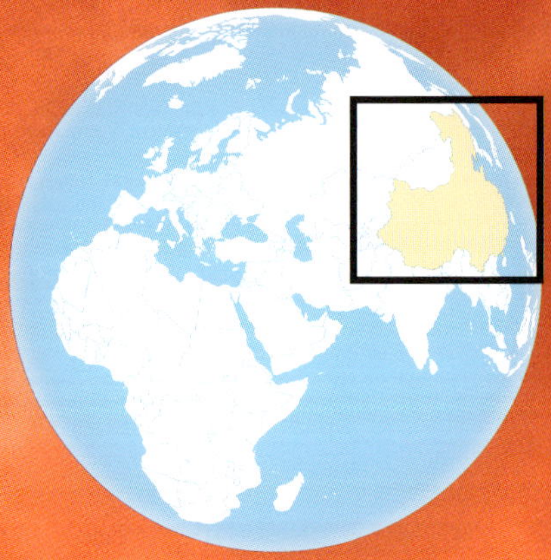

climate change.[10] Smog, deforestation, and overgrazing have sped up this process, which is called desertification. This has led to worsened air quality. More frequent dust storms have stirred up a toxic mix of heavy metals, viruses, bacteria, and pesticides. The loss has forced people to move and is shrinking agricultural land reserves.

China's three major plains run from north to south along the northeast and eastern seaboard. Although prone to flooding, the plains have mild temperatures, fertile soils, and relatively flat terrain. Eleven percent of China's land is arable, and most of it is within these three major plains.[11] Major crops grown in the Northeast Plain include soybeans, flax, and rice. Wheat, maize, peanuts, and cotton are grown in the North China Plain. The Middle-Lower Yangtze Plain has rolling hills, streams, rivers, and lakes. The region is a major source of fish, shrimp, and water chestnuts. Rice, cotton, and silk are also grown here.

The country's famous rice terraces are in southwest China. The Honghe Hani Rice Terraces in southern Yunnan have been designated a UNESCO World Heritage site. The people of the region have been developing these 41,027 acres (16,603 ha)

YANGTZE RIVER

At 3,915 miles (6,300 km), the Yangtze River (Chang Jiang) is the longest river in Asia and the third-longest river in the world.[12] From its source in the Tibetan Plateau, it flows east across the southern part of the country to the East China Sea. The Yangtze River delta is among the most densely populated regions in the country. Some of China's largest cities are found here, including Shanghai, the nation's most populous city. It is the major waterway in China, connecting inland cities with the seaports. Luxury river cruises are a popular tourist attraction along the river.

Parts of the Gobi desert are sandy, but other areas are rocky. Many notable fossils have been uncovered in the Gobi desert.

of land for 1,300 years.[13] They built a complex system of channels to bring fresh water from the mountains to the terraces. The terraces support not only the primary crop, red rice, but also an agricultural system that includes buffalo, cattle, ducks, and fish.

CLIMATE AND SEASONS

China is located entirely in the Northern Hemisphere, so its seasons occur at the same time of year as in the United States. However, its vast size and diverse geography contribute to big differences in climate from region to region. The Yangtze River acts as a natural divide between the northern and southern parts of the country. In the north, temperatures can dip well below freezing. In the winter months, the region's weather is overcast and generally hovers around –4 degrees Fahrenheit (–20°C). In the summer, the northern region is wet and warm. It can

The stunning Honghe Hani Rice Terraces are tended by people living in 82 nearby villages.

Summer monsoon rains generally reach Chengdu in central China by early July.

YELLOW MOUNTAIN

Found in Anhui province, Mount Huang, also known as Yellow Mountain, often comes to mind when people think of scenic Chinese landscapes. It has been depicted in art and literature since the 700s CE. Rocky peaks, some more than 3,280 feet (1,000 m) high, slice through the cloud line and pop up on the other side, making their tops look like floating islands in the sky.[17] Often called the loveliest mountain in China, its jutting rock formations and ancient, gnarled trees inspired the *shan shui* school of landscape painting that is popular throughout China. *Shan shui* means "mountain and water."

reach 100 degrees Fahrenheit (38°C). The most pleasant temperatures in this region are in the spring months of April and May and in the fall months of September and October, when average temperatures range between 68 and 86 degrees Fahrenheit (20–30°C).[14]

The southeast region of China experiences monsoon rainfall in the summer months, with some cities receiving as much as 12 inches (30 cm) of rain in both June and July.[15] It can also be warm and humid in the southeast in the summer, with temperatures reaching as high as 104 degrees Fahrenheit (40°C). The winter in the southeast is mild, with an average temperature of approximately 50 degrees Fahrenheit (10°C).[16] Central and western China experience many floods and significant seismic activity.

CHAPTER **THREE**

PLANTS AND ANIMALS

China's vast mountain ranges, long coastline, extensive river system, and massive deserts create habitats for a wide range of plants and animals. Logging, mineral extraction, illegal hunting, the wildlife trade, pollution, and climate change have all threatened species' habitats. In 2021, China updated its list of National Key Protected Wild Animals for the first time since 1989, adding 500 species to the list.[1] Since the mid-1990s, the Chinese government has worked to manage some of these problems by creating more protected green spaces, addressing pollution, and considering natural habitats in development plans. But a demand for wildlife

Giant pandas have become symbols of China, and after development caused populations to decline, Chinese authorities launched intensive conservation efforts.

products still drove the global trade of endangered species parts like rhino horns and tiger bones.

ANIMALS

China is home to unusual animals of all shapes and sizes, from the world's smallest snail to its largest salamander. There are 551 mammal species in China.[2] China's best-known animal is the giant panda, which lives in the mountainous bamboo forests of the country's southwest. Large animals such as Asiatic black bears, goatlike mammals called takins, and Siberian ibexes also live among China's mountains. Asian elephants, an endangered species, live in the foothills and forests of the southwest region of the country.

China's rivers are also home to unique animals. The waters and areas along riverbanks are home to alligators, salamanders, eels, and many species of fish. Water deer graze in the tall reeds and rushes. The world's largest amphibian, the Chinese giant

SAVING GIANT PANDAS

Giant pandas once lived throughout southern and eastern China. Development and hunting caused their numbers to dwindle. By the 1980s, there were only approximately 1,000 giant pandas remaining in the wild.[3] To save them, the Chinese government worked with the World Wildlife Federation to preserve more than 53,000 square miles (137,000 sq km) of habitat.[4] Conservation workers developed bamboo corridors, stretches of forest that connected isolated areas of panda habitat. This allowed the pandas to roam safely. China also created the Giant Panda National Park. It encompasses 70 percent of the panda's existing habitat. In 2017, the International Union for the Conservation of Nature (IUCN) changed the giant panda's status from endangered to vulnerable. It is estimated there are now 1,850 giant pandas living in the wild.[5] An additional 633 are in captive breeding programs.[6]

Chinese giant salamanders can grow to nearly six feet (1.8 m) in length.

salamander, lives in the Yangtze River along with the Chinese alligator. The giant salamander is critically endangered because of overharvesting for human consumption. Chinese alligators are also threatened. There are as few as 120 left.[7] Their habitat has been fragmented, and their food sources have been contaminated by pesticides.

The seas of China are also home to diverse species. In the waters off Hong Kong, a small population of endangered Indo-Pacific humpback dolphins survives, but it is at risk. These dolphins are white or pink and attract tourists. High-speed ferries between Macao and Hong Kong are one of the threats the dolphins face. Dugongs, also known as sea cows, long struggled to survive off the southern coast, and in 2022 scientists declared them extinct in China.

The coastline of the Yellow Sea is a migratory route for more than 500 species of birds. The coastal wetlands of the Yellow Sea are an important feeding ground for these birds. Development of the coast has robbed the birds of habitat and food, putting 10 percent of the birds that use this route at risk of extinction. To address the problem, China's State Oceanic Administration introduced several conservation initiatives, including establishing 16 new marine parks in 2016. This move brought the country's total protected marine areas to about 48,000 square miles (124,000 sq km).[8]

China's desert is a critical habitat for many endangered animals. These include the Bactrian camel, which is the last wild camel; Przewalski's

POACHING FOR MEDICINE

Traditional Chinese medicine (TCM) uses 36 animal species in its remedies. Loss of habitat and increasing demand for TCM from a growing population have put these species at risk. As a result, many wild animals are poached, or hunted illegally. In 1993, China banned the tiger bone trade, but a 2006 survey revealed that 3 percent of medicine shops still carried them. The rhino is a protected species, but poaching remains lucrative because of its use in TCM. Approximately 20 million seahorses are harvested every year to supply the TCM industry.[9] Although not endangered, they are at risk.

horse, the only wild horse that has never been domesticated; and the snow leopard. Loss of habitat from development and illegal hunting have threatened these and other animals in China.

THE DAWN REDWOOD

The dawn redwood is one of only three redwood species in the world. Abundant across the Northern Hemisphere 50 million to 100 million years ago, it was thought to be extinct for millions of years. In 1946, a group from the Save the Redwoods League traveled to China and located a few thousand dawn redwoods. Unlike other redwoods, the dawn redwood is deciduous, not evergreen. It sheds its leaves every fall, is bare all winter, and then grows new foliage in the spring. There are only a few areas in China where it grows naturally. The IUCN has listed it as endangered, and it is a protected species in China.

FORESTS, TREES, AND PLANTS

In 1949, only 8.6 percent of China was forested.[10] Deforestation for lumber and development stripped the country of much of its forested area. Extensive reforestation programs in the 1950s and 1970s increased forestation. More aggressive measures since the 1990s have also helped. By 2020, 23 percent of the country was forested. China set a goal to achieve 30 percent forest cover by 2050.[11]

China's foliage varies from one region to the next. China has boreal, subtropical, and tropical forests. The boreal forest runs along the country's northern borders with Mongolia and Russia. It is composed mostly of coniferous trees such as pines, spruces, and firs. Mosses, fungi, and lichens grow beneath the towering evergreens of the boreal forest.

Jiuzhai Valley, located in southwest China's Sichuan province, is home to important forest ecosystems.

China's subtropical forests extend from the southeast part of the country to northern Vietnam. Laurels, beeches, chestnuts, oaks, mahoganies, and mangroves grow in these forests. In southwest China, the Xishuangbanna Biosphere Reserve is the country's largest tropical rainforest. The reserve is home to an incredible variety of plant life. It contains more than 2,700 species of plants, including more than 260 species of ferns.[12]

Plant life in China's deserts has adapted to its arid environment. The Gobi desert has saxaul trees, wild onions, sophora, and a type of white flowering bindweed. Wetter areas also have plants that have adapted to thrive in local conditions. Along the Yangtze River basin, Chinese willow trees, dove trees, and bamboo plants grow. Lotus blossoms and chrysanthemums brighten the river shores with their colorful petals.

China has 34 UNESCO-designated biosphere reserves, places where conservation authorities test new approaches to preserving biodiversity.[13]

Parks in large urban areas, such as Shanghai, provide spaces for recreation and relaxation amid big-city life.

PARKS AND GREEN SPACES

At the beginning of the 2000s, China started to transform its cities, adding green spaces, gardens, and outdoor areas for people to enjoy. A government push to increase urban green spaces saw these areas grow by nearly five times between 2001 and 2021. The COVID-19 outbreak, which began in late 2019 and was declared a pandemic in 2020, sped up the government's park development. In 2020, Shanghai opened 55 new parks, bringing its total to 406. The city of Suzhou opened 20 new parks in 2020 and 2021, and another city, Kaifeng, opened 28.[14] In March 2021, the Chinese government approved a five-year plan that included a nationwide program to develop urban parks.

China is home to 225 national parks.[15] To gain national park status, a park must have historic or scenic importance. Established in 1982, the Zhangjiajie National Forest Park, located in Hunan province in central China, was the country's first national park. It is distinguished by approximately 3,000 sandstone columns that line gorges, ravines, and waterfalls. Lushan National Park, found in Jiangxi province in southeast-central China, spans 74,626 acres (30,200 ha) of mountains, caves, lakes, and botanical gardens.[16] In Yunnan province in southern China, the Shilin Stone Forest is famous for its limestone formations. The stones have eroded over 270 million years, creating a display of massive pillars emerging from the ground.[17]

At 122,008 square miles (316,000 sq km) in area and 13,123 feet (4,000 m) in elevation, the Sanjiangyuan Nature Reserve is China's largest and highest nature reserve.[18]

CHAPTER **FOUR**

HISTORY

The fossils of human ancestors found in China date back hundreds of thousands of years. Archaeologists have uncovered stone tools, food storage vessels, and evidence of complex societies from the 5000s BCE. A variety of cultures established themselves in different parts of what is now China. Tales of legendary figures, events, and dynasties are intertwined with the earliest Chinese history. But the first ruling dynasty to leave written records dates to approximately 1600 BCE.

THE IMPERIAL DYNASTIES

Thirteen major imperial dynasties ruled China over a span of 3,500 years. Imperial dynasties are ruling families that pass power down the hereditary line,

In June 2022, researchers carefully analyzed artifacts at the Sanxingdui Ruins site in Sichuan, China. Objects at these ruins date back as far as 4,500 years.

usually from father to son. Most historians consider the Shang dynasty, which ruled the Huang He valley starting in approximately 1600 BCE, to mark the beginning of Chinese culture. Many early historians believed the earlier Xia dynasty was a myth created by the Shang dynasty, but excavations in the 1900s uncovered artifacts corresponding to this time period.

A tribal king named Tang was the Shang dynasty's first ruler. There was an established class structure in the dynasty, with the king, nobles, and appointed governors at the top and the working masses below. The people worked in agriculture, and the king would tell them when to plant seeds and harvest crops. They became so proficient at growing that they moved beyond subsistence farming, freeing up workers to build infrastructure. Inscriptions on tortoiseshell discovered from this period are the earliest known Chinese writing. The Shang dynasty had been in power for almost 600 years under 30 different kings when the Zhou dynasty overthrew it in 1046 BCE.

THE TERRA-COTTA ARMY

On March 29, 1974, a farmer in China's Shaanxi province dug up the first piece of what would become one of the greatest archaeological finds of the 1900s. Buried next to the tomb of Emperor Qin Shi Huang was a complete life-size army made from terra-cotta. Approximately 2,000 warriors have been unburied so far. Each is unique, with a different facial expression, pose, and real weapon, and they are organized in battle formation by rank with their clothing identifying their roles as infantry, archers, charioteers, or officers. Archaeologists have uncovered horses, chariots, musicians, acrobats, and even cranes and ducks. It is thought there could be up to 6,000 more statues still buried.[1]

The Zhou dynasty ruled for eight centuries, the longest of the dynasties. It controlled the area north of the Huang He to the Yangtze River in eastern China. The Zhou did not wield control from a place of central power. Instead, there were up to 200 states ruled by family members of the king. This connected the states through kinship, which made it easy to share ideas, resources, and technology.

Over time, kinship alliances weakened, and conflict broke out during the Warring States period (475–221 BCE). Conflict continued between these states until 221 BCE, when the Qin dynasty conquered all the states and took control of China. The Qin dynasty was one of the shortest of the imperial dynasties. It ruled from 221 BCE to 207 BCE. The first ruler named himself Qin Shi Huang, which translates to "First Emperor of Qin." With military might, he brought the warring states together to form the nation

Tang, the first leader of the Shang dynasty, was said to have been the descendent of a mythical Chinese leader.

now known as China. Shi Huang tore down all the border walls that separated states and built one enormous wall along the northern border of his empire. This would become the Great Wall of China. He implemented a common currency, script, and set of measurements. He also ordered the construction of an approximately 500-mile (800 km) highway called the Straight Road that was used to transport material to build the Great Wall.[2]

Shi Huang's son succeeded him upon his death in 210 BCE. Two years later, he was overthrown by warlord Xiang Yu. Xiang Yu executed the emperor and divided the empire into 18 states. Liu Bang ruled the Han River valley. He battled Xiang Yu for three years for control of the full empire. In 202 BCE, Xiang Yu died by suicide and Liu Bang became emperor of the new Han dynasty. Its capital was Chang'an in western China.

The Han established centralized systems for providing services and conducting business. They expanded Chinese territory and built a network of trade routes that connected China and the Far East with the Middle East and Europe. Now commonly called the Silk Road, this network also brought foreign religions, such as Buddhism, to China. The Han dynasty ruled for more than 400 years.

GREAT WALL OF CHINA

Built over 2,000 years by several dynasties to fortify their kingdoms, the Great Wall of China is a series of smaller walls that, together, are more than 13,000 miles (20,900 km) long. The most well-known section was built during the Ming dynasty. It is 5,500 miles (8,851 km) long, running east to west across northern China. The wall varies in height from 15 feet (4.6 m) to 39 feet (11.9 m) and is 32 feet (9.8 m) wide at its thickest point. Every year, ten million people visit the wall, which was named a UNESCO World Heritage site in 1987.[3]

However, it was divided into separate kingdoms by rival warlords. The Han dynasty ended when warlord Cao Pi forced the last emperor, Xian, to give up his throne in 220 CE.

THE SILK ROAD

The trade routes between China and Greece opened during the Han dynasty. The routes were not given the name "Silk Road" until 1877, when a German geographer used the term to describe the overland routes because silk was among the most valuable items traded on them. Some historians prefer the term "Silk Routes" because it more accurately reflects the multitude of land and maritime passages that formed the trade routes. The Silk Routes included a network of trading posts and markets where goods were stored and traded. Goods such as Chinese silk and gunpowder traveled west, while wool, gold, and silver came east to China. A section of paved highway that in modern times connects Pakistan to Xinjiang, China, was once part of the Silk Road.

TURBULENCE AND REBELLION

The next 350 years were turbulent for China. The period from 220 to 589 was known as the Six Dynasties period. In the south, six successive Chinese dynasties ruled from the capital Jianye, which is present-day Nanjing. The north was ruled by a succession of dynasties from East Asia that divided the region into many states controlled by warlords.

The north and south remained divided until 589. The Six Dynasties period ended when a military commander in the north, Yang Jian, seized control of the government, united the north, and then captured the south's capital of Nanjing. Within three months, the south had fallen, and the country was united.

Emperor Wendi, *second from right*, reunified the country after a long period of division. His reign was marked by peace and prosperity.

Yang Jian became Emperor Wendi. He named the new dynasty Sui, after his father. The Sui dynasty built a new capital city called Daxing in nine months. The second Sui emperor, Yangdi, built a second capital, Luoyang, in the east. However, many of his construction projects were expensive, he engaged in several failed military operations, and he lived an extravagant lifestyle. Yangdi bankrupted the country. This led to the downfall of the Sui dynasty.

In 618, an army general named Li Yuan led a rebellion and took control of the country. He founded the Tang dynasty and became Emperor Gaozu. The Tang oversaw a united and flourishing empire for almost 300 years. This dynasty expanded its territory to the Korean peninsula in the east, Mongolia in the north, Vietnam in the south, and Afghanistan in the west. Cities along the Silk Road became global trading hubs. Under the Tang, China became the most powerful empire in the world. Gunpowder and timekeeping devices were invented in China during this time. The dynasty began to crumble in 907 when the warlord Zhu Wen assassinated the last emperor, Zhaozong. The assassin installed Zhaozong's 11-year-old son Ai as emperor. Zhu then ordered Ai assassinated when he was 15, ending the Tang dynasty for good. For the next 50 years, China would be thrown into a period of unrest while warlords from various states fought for power. In 960, the Song dynasty came to power. It would remain in power until 1279. The economy boomed, with merchants exporting paper, silk, rice, tea, and copper. Horses, sheep, cotton, gems, and spices were imported.

China's only female ruler, Empress Wuhou, was in power from 683 to 704 CE during the Tang dynasty.

MONGOL INVASION AND THE LAST IMPERIAL DYNASTY

In 1273, Mongol leader Kublai Khan invaded the city of Xiangyang. In 1275, he crossed the Yangtze River and slaughtered the people of Changzhou. By 1279, he had completely defeated the Song dynasty. The Mongols set up the Yuan dynasty. China became part of the Mongol empire, which covered one-fifth of the world's land at the time.[4] Kublai Khan was the first Yuan

Large surviving portions of the Great Wall were constructed during the Ming dynasty.

ruler of all of China. Beijing became the capital for the first time. However, the Mongolian Yuan never assimilated with the native Chinese. Yuan rulers brought in outsiders to hold bureaucratic positions. Revolts against the Yuan rulers began in the mid-1300s. In 1368, Zhu Yuanzhang, a leader of the rebel group known as the White Lotus society, captured Beijing. That same year, the Yuan dynasty was overthrown. It had been in power for less than 100 years. Zhu Yuanzhang destroyed the palaces and announced the creation of the Ming dynasty.

The Ming dynasty ruled from 1368 to 1644. During that time, the population of China doubled. The Forbidden City was built in the 1400s during Ming rule. In time, rival factions began forming among the civil officials. This, combined with a weak emperor, left an opening for rebel leader Li Zicheng to capture Beijing. The Ming asked for military support from the Manchu tribal people who lived along China's northern border. They helped drive out Li Zicheng but then took the country as their own. In 1644, the Manchu formed the Qing dynasty.

The Qing dynasty would be the last imperial dynasty of China. It ruled from 1644 to 1912. During this time, the population grew from 150 million to 450 million people.[5] The empire grew to include outer Mongolia, Tibet, Turkistan, and Nepal. It ruled more than five million square miles (13 million sq km) of land.[6] The Qing dynasty's influence spread beyond China's borders. Through trade and migrant Chinese laborers, it also exerted power in the port cities of what are now the Philippines, Malaysia, and Indonesia. The dynasty continued to thrive until the late 1700s, when floods, famine, and the demands of a fast-growing population led to unrest and rebellions. The army was also in a weakened state due to poor leadership.

In 1839, the Qing entered the first of two Opium Wars. British traders had been bringing illegal, addictive opium from India into China for years, but in the early 1800s, the volume soared. The Chinese government tried to confiscate a massive cache of opium that British merchants had stored in the city of Guangzhou. The First Opium War (1839–1842) began in September 1839. The British brought a fleet of ships up the Pearl River and occupied cities. After losing several battles and the failure of a major counterattack in early 1842, China entered peace talks with the British in August 1842. Signed on August 29, 1842, the Treaty of Nanjing would be the first in a long line of unequal treaties. In it, China agreed to pay Britain compensation, give up Hong Kong, and increase the number of ports where the British could dock and trade. Included among these ports was Shanghai, which would become a major trading center.

During the First Opium War, technological advantages helped the British defeat Chinese forces both at sea and on land.

By fall of 1856, the Chinese and British were embroiled in the Second Opium War (1856–1860). In October 1856, a British warship sailed up the Pearl River and bombed Guangzhou. In December, the Chinese burned all the foreign trading warehouses in Guangzhou. Soon the French joined the British. In late 1857, the two allied countries captured the city. Once again, the Chinese made concessions to the foreign invaders. The British, French, and Chinese signed the treaties of Tianjin in June 1858. Foreign diplomats were granted residence in Beijing, even more ports were opened to Western trade, and importing opium to China was legalized.

China had long exerted control over Korea. However, Korea's wealth of natural resources also made it attractive to Japan. The Qing fought against Japan for control of Korea in the Sino-Japanese War (1894–1895). Japan was victorious, and China signed another in a long line of peace treaties that required it to pay money, give trading privileges to a foreign country, and cede territory, in this case Taiwan.

By the end of the 1800s, poverty, a series of natural disasters, and the foreign exploitation of their country were causing widespread frustration among the Chinese. A secret society called the Righteous and Harmonious Fists formed. Foreigners called them Boxers after the boxing and exercise rituals they practiced. The Boxer Rebellion started in 1899 when this society wanted to overthrow the imperial dynasty and privileged foreigners in China. The Boxers gained strength in northern China, invaded Chinese cities, and killed foreigners.

Western nations offered to send help to the Chinese, but the Qing dynasty decided to work with the Boxers instead. The Boxers dropped their opposition to the dynasty and joined it to fight the foreigners. The Qing dynasty

Troops from Western nations occupied the Imperial Palace in Beijing during the Boxer Rebellion.

declared war on the Western nations. A force of 19,000 Japanese, Russian, British, US, French, Austro-Hungarian, and Italian troops was assembled to fight the Chinese.[7]

Western forces defeated the Imperial Army in 1901, killing Boxers and anyone in the Qing government who supported them. A new emperor, Xuantong, took the throne, but the dynasty had lost its power. With the support of Qing imperial soldiers, the Nationalist Party held an uprising in 1911. Fifteen provinces declared their independence from the empire. This forced the Qing to agree to create the new Republic of China. Xuantong gave up the throne in 1912, ending more than 3,500 years of imperial rule in China.

DECADES OF WAR

The Republic of China was unstable, and the next several decades were full of political turmoil and war. At the start of World War I (1914–1918), China declared neutrality. But Germany's largest overseas naval base was in the Shandong Peninsula of China, and Japan's opposing forces plotted to capture it. Japanese and British troops crossed Chinese territory to launch their attack, imposing on China's neutrality. China joined the war in 1917 to ensure it had an influence on treaty negotiations so it could advocate for its own control over occupied Chinese territories. However, when the Treaty of Versailles was negotiated at the end of the war, the leading victorious nations sided with Japan and granted it continued control over the Shandong Peninsula.

On May 4, 1919, Chinese students launched a protest against Japanese control of Chinese territory. Two rival groups, the Nationalist Party and the Chinese Communist Party (CCP), gained power and influence in the wake of this discontent. The Nationalist Party established control of the country in 1928. In opposition, the CCP built up its strength from bases in rural China. But in 1937, when Japan invaded China, the groups set aside their differences and joined to fight the invaders. World War II (1939–1945) broke out in Europe in 1939, and the United States entered the war in 1941. China's allies, including the Soviet Union and the United States, provided military aid. The Japanese invasion and occupation of China were brutal, and millions of soldiers and civilians were killed. The defeat of Japan in 1945 ended the war, and the Japanese occupiers were driven out of China.

THE CHINESE WORKFORCE OF WORLD WAR I

In 1914, officially neutral China secretly offered 50,000 troops to the British to help retake the city of Qingdao in Shandong from Germany.[8] The British refused. Instead, Britain-allied Japan occupied the region for the duration of the war. Japan also opposed China joining the war, so instead of sending combat troops, the Chinese sent voluntary noncombat workers to help the war effort without officially losing China's neutral status. Tens of thousands of Chinese workers went to France, the United Kingdom, and Russia to repair tanks, assemble artillery shells, transport supplies, and dig trenches.

THE PEOPLE'S REPUBLIC OF CHINA

The end of World War II did not end conflict in China. After the victory against Japan, the Nationalists and the CCP resumed their civil war. In 1949, Mao Zedong, the leader of the CCP, declared victory and established the communist-led People's Republic of China (PRC). The Nationalists retreated

Chinese Nationalist leader Chiang Kai-Shek, *left*, met with US president Franklin D. Roosevelt, *center*, and British prime minister Winston Churchill, *right*, to plan war strategy against the Japanese in 1943.

to the island of Taiwan. The United States did not recognize the new communist regime and cut all formal ties with the government. It instead continued to recognize the Nationalists in Taiwan as the rulers of China.

The establishment of the PRC was the beginning of massive political, cultural, and economic change for China. Mao expelled foreigners from the country, consolidated central power, and rebuilt a nation broken and struggling after decades of war. He adopted a communist system for

China whereby all members of society would share in the nation's wealth and resources. However, his government was also an authoritarian dictatorship that oppressed those who opposed his regime. The regime cracked down on corruption and criminal activity that had stalled economic development. Mao introduced policies that significantly harmed the Chinese people. His Great Leap Forward program, meant to industrialize the country, disrupted agriculture and caused mass starvation, killing millions. The Cultural Revolution, meant to increase loyalty to the party's ideals, led to radicalized CCP forces terrorizing people and launching purges of those seen to be disloyal.

After Mao died in 1976, Chinese leader Deng Xiaoping sought to improve China's fortunes by opening the country to Western nations. The result was one of the biggest economic reforms in history. In 1978, more than three-quarters of all Chinese rural people lived in poverty.[9] In the 1980s, Deng introduced many policies that grew the Chinese economy and lifted people out of poverty. One example was the household responsibility system, in which individual farming households gained more freedom to manage agricultural land as they saw necessary. Deng also established special economic zones such as Shenzhen and Xiamen, where foreign companies could trade and do business with less bureaucracy than in other regions. China was improving economically, but demands for political reforms and greater social freedoms grew in the late 1980s, reaching a peak with the bloody suppression of the Tiananmen Square protests in June 1989.

In response to the unrest, the government took firmer control of politics and culture, but economic reforms continued through the 1990s. President Hu Jintao oversaw continued growth in the early 2000s, and President Xi Jinping took power in 2013. China's economic and military power

A photo of a lone protester standing before a column of tanks became an enduring symbol of the 1989 Tiananmen Square protests. The image and any discussion of the protester are subject to censorship within China.

kept growing under Xi, and his policies, known as Xi Jinping Thought, became a core part of the CCP's ideology and were incorporated into the nation's education system. In 2018, the government eliminated term limits for the presidency, making it possible for Xi to remain president for life.

MINI **BIO**

MAO ZEDONG

Mao Zedong was a soldier who led China's communist revolution. He was the leader and chairman of the CCP from 1935 until his death in 1976. He was also the chairman of the PRC from 1949 to 1959. Mao was the architect of two policies that profoundly affected the country. In 1958, he introduced the Great Leap Forward policy, which led to a food shortage. By 1962, it is estimated that more than 20 million people died of starvation.[10]

Mao became concerned that China was straying from his vision of communism, so he encouraged the youth to reinforce his values. In 1966, Mao launched a program called the Cultural Revolution. He called for students to attack traditional values, including what were called the Four Olds: old culture, customs, habits of mind, and ideas. The students Mao mobilized, known as the Red Guards, attacked elderly people, scholars, and others. It is believed that between 500,000 and two million people died as a result.[11]

The Chinese government has acknowledged Mao's mistakes, especially later in his life, but also celebrates his accomplishments in the creation of modern China.

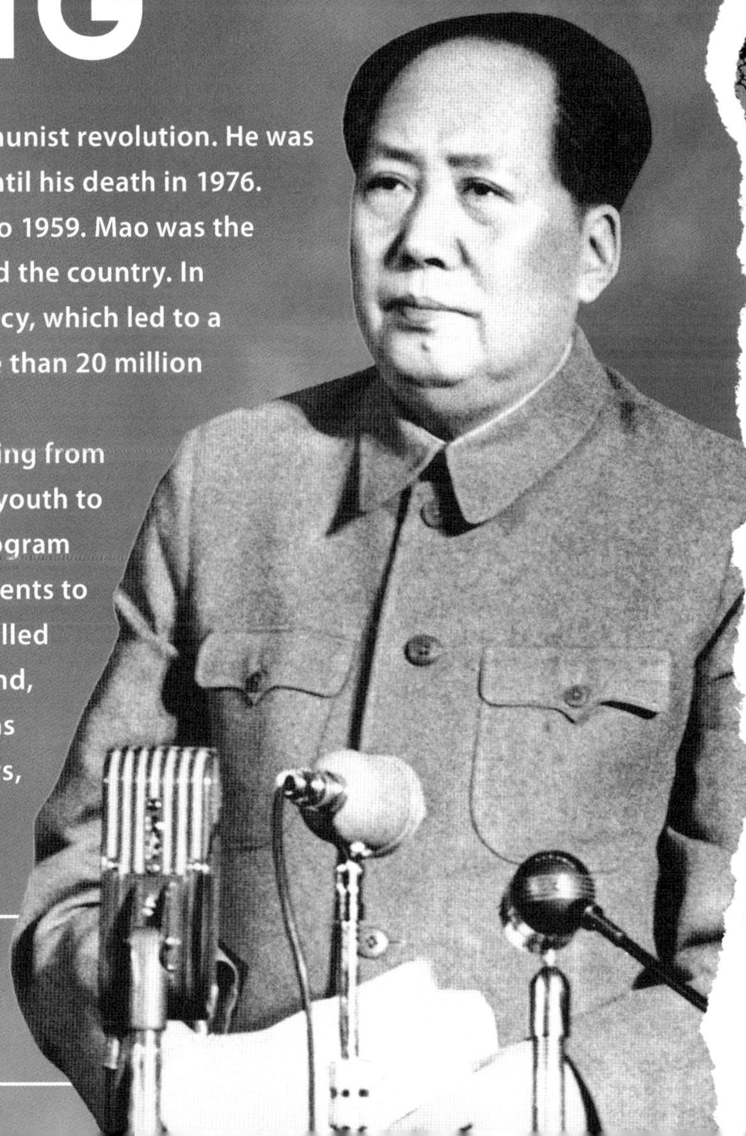

CHAPTER **FIVE**

PEOPLE AND CULTURE

China's long history and immense size make it impossible to define its people as a single group. Customs vary among regions and ethnic groups, creating a rich assortment of traditions. It is a country where people respect and continue long-standing cultural practices while also adhering to modern ideas and influences.

DEMOGRAPHICS

China's population is almost completely ethnically Chinese, with 91 percent of the population being Han Chinese. Nine percent of the population are ethnic minorities, including the Uighur Manchu, Tibetan, and Mongol people. In all, China recognizes 56 ethnic

China's vast population means that even though Han Chinese form a significant majority, more than 100 million people belong to ethnic minority groups.

minority groups.[1] With more than 1.4 billion citizens in 2022, China is the most populated country in the world.[2]

In 1980, in response to a sharply rising population, the Chinese government implemented a one-child policy for most couples. Thirty-five years later, with an aging population, the government lifted the one-child policy and put in place a two-child policy. The country completed a survey in 2020 and discovered that 2.65 million fewer babies were born in 2020 than in 2019.[3] In 2021, the government announced it would allow couples to have three children. Because of China's low birthrate, the country's population growth had almost stalled by 2021. The median age of the Chinese population was 38.4 years, meaning a large number of people would reach retirement age over the next few decades.[4]

Most of China's population lives in huge urban centers in the eastern portion of the country. Since the end of the 1940s, the growth of urban centers has been significant. China had 69 cities at the end of the 1940s. By 2007, that number had ballooned to 670, with 89 cities having populations of more than one million.[5] By 2022, it had 160 cities with populations of more than one million. Five cities, including Shanghai and Beijing, had more than ten million people each.[6]

LANGUAGES

Since 1930, the official language of the country has been Mandarin. Many other dialects are spoken in the country, though. Mandarin itself is a dialect of the group of Chinese Sino-Tibetan languages. Mandarin has dialects of its own, and these can be broken into subdialects. Unlike dialects

Hangzhou, China's eleventh-largest city, has more people than Los Angeles and Chicago combined.

of English, which all English speakers can usually understand, dialects of Chinese can differ significantly from one another. For example, someone who speaks Mandarin cannot necessarily understand someone who speaks Cantonese, the language spoken in Hong Kong. Cantonese is another dialect of the Chinese Sino-Tibetan languages. Seventy percent of Chinese people speak Mandarin.[7]

Bilingual schools in Xinjiang teach Mandarin to Uighur students.

Some self-governed regions have their own official languages. Uighur is the official language of Xinjiang. Tibetan is the official language of Tibet, and Mongolian is the official language of Inner Mongolia. Most children now also learn English in school.

RELIGION

Both religion and philosophy have had a major influence on China's culture. Chinese people have practiced Buddhism and Taoism since the early imperial dynasties, and Confucianism was adopted as an official philosophy by the Han dynasty. However, when the CCP formed the PRC in 1949, it declared the country an atheist nation. Several religions are still practiced in China, though. The three most common are folk religion, Buddhism, and Christianity. Despite religious freedom in the constitution, many religious groups are persecuted by the government. The government is known to monitor religious activities and undertakes annual inspections of religious organizations. Groups are dispersed and arbitrarily fined. They may have their property seized, and members are sometimes detained. In the Xinjiang region, the Chinese government has detained more than one million Muslim Uighurs and sent them to reeducation camps with the stated purpose of combating religious extremism. Leaked police documents suggested a policy of shooting those who tried to escape the camps.

Twenty-two percent of the population practices Chinese folk religion.[8] What folk religion encompasses and how people practice folk religion varies from region to region. It is a blend of Confucianism, Taoism, Buddhism, shamanism, ancestor worship, animism, and magic. A little more than half the population claims no religious affiliation, but many of these people might still practice a Chinese folk religion. Buddhism is the second most-practiced religion, with 18.2 percent of Chinese people identifying as Buddhist.[9] Christianity is practiced by about 5 percent of the population.[10] This number is quickly rising. During the Cultural Revolution, the government repressed Christianity. But since 1979, the number of Protestant Christians in China has grown by 10 percent annually. It is estimated that China could have the world's largest population of Christians by 2030.[11]

Members of the Christian minority in China celebrated Easter at a candlelight mass in 2021.

FESTIVALS AND HOLIDAYS

People in China celebrate seven national holidays, including New Year's Day, Chinese New Year, the Qingming Festival, May Day, the Dragon Boat Festival, Mid-Autumn Festival, and National Day. Also known as the Spring Festival and Lunar New Year, Chinese New Year is the biggest celebration of the year. The seven-day holiday celebrates the Lunar New Year and the approaching spring and has long held cultural significance for the Chinese. During the holiday, people light red lanterns, give family members money in red envelopes, set off fireworks, hold parades with dragon dances, and host parties and banquets.

Another major celebration is National Day, which begins on October 1 each year. The holiday commemorates when the PRC was founded, and celebrations continue for seven days. This is called the Golden Week. Many people travel to visit family or go on vacation. Since 2015, traffic jams around major cities have become a tremendous problem during Golden Week.

CHINESE PORCELAIN

In English, porcelain is sometimes called "china" because it was first invented in China. Porcelain is fired at a higher temperature, is more transparent, and has greater luster than other types of pottery. Early forms of porcelain first appeared during the Shang dynasty, but the fine porcelain China is famous for was not produced until the Han dynasty. Since then, each period of China's history has left its own distinctive mark on the art form. Many porcelain artifacts, such as vases from the Ming dynasty, are worth millions of dollars. In 2021, a vase from the 1700s sold at an auction for $41.6 million.[12]

ART AND ARCHITECTURE

Poetry, literature, opera, painting, porcelain, jade, and bronze are just some of the arts that have been made in China for centuries. Among the nation's oldest and most well-known artistic forms are calligraphy, silk painting, and embroidery. Calligraphy is a pen-lettering art form that made its way into the imperial court during the Han dynasty. Poetry and calligraphy were a shared art form, as poetry was written in calligraphy. Educated people were expected to master calligraphy, and the elite enjoyed writing and reading poetry.

Silk played an important role in China following its invention in 3600 BCE. People wrote their calligraphy on silk before paper was invented. The fine, smooth textile was also used for painting. Silk painting evolved from the simple black brushstrokes of calligraphy to include vibrant colors

Examples of classic Chinese architectural styles, such as the Pavilion of Prince Teng in Nanchang, can be found among modern buildings in Chinese cities. The pavilion has been destroyed and rebuilt multiple times over the centuries.

and more lifelike depictions. People have also used the material for embroidery since the Han dynasty. Seamstresses delicately stitch brightly colored silk threads through a silk background fabric to create beautiful images.

China's unique architecture, ranging from ancient buildings to modern skyscrapers, reflects Chinese culture. Ancient Chinese architecture was designed to withstand natural disasters, such as earthquakes and floods. People built with wood because of its flexibility and availability. Ceramic tiled roofs with wide eaves were also a distinctive feature of Chinese buildings. Wide overhanging roofs were important to protect wood buildings from rotting in the rain. They also provided shade in the summer.

Ancient Chinese buildings followed rules regarding orientation, layout, and design. People built structures facing south, with lower buildings in front and taller buildings behind. This allowed for maximum sunlight to heat and light the space during the gloomy, cold winter months. Windows and doors of the main building faced south and opened to the inner courtyard. The main building of a compound would sit in the center, with smaller buildings surrounding it on all sides. This design protected the most important building from the weather, and it also provided defense against attacks.

The National Stadium's saddle-shaped steel exterior measures 1,093 feet (333 m) north to south, 965 feet (294 m) east to west, and 227 feet (69 m) tall.[14]

Since the 1980s, China has become more open to the outside world, and with this shift has come more diverse architecture. Urban centers are packed with modern skyscrapers. One of the country's most iconic structures is the National Stadium, which was built for the 2008 Olympic Games in Beijing. The stadium is also known as the Bird's Nest. An architectural marvel, it cost $480 million to build and seats 91,000 people.[13] It was the largest enclosed space in the world when it was built.

FOOD AND DINING

In urban centers, breakfast is a quick meal before school or work. It might include rice porridge, steamed buns, or deep-fried dough sticks called *youtiao*. Some regions have dim sum for brunch.

It is a leisurely meal where small servings of dumplings, fried and braised chicken feet, and other bite-size foods are served with tea.

Lunch is often simple, with a small serving of rice or noodles and meat or vegetables. Dinner is the main meal of the day. The meal will include soup, rice or noodles, meats, and vegetables. Many recipes feature a five-spice blend called wu xiang fen, which typically includes fennel seeds, cinnamon, clove, Sichuan pepper, and star anise. Families come together to enjoy the meal. If people go out to a restaurant, they will often stay and socialize or play games after they have finished eating.

Some foods are linked with particular festivals. Baked treats called moon cakes are traditionally made for the Mid-Autumn Festival. Families give, receive, and enjoy these pastries containing sweet filling around a salted duck egg yolk.

SHARK FIN SOUP

Shark fin soup has long been a traditional dish at special occasions in China, such as weddings. But the dish became so popular that it threatened global shark populations. Fins from millions of sharks are used for the soup every year. Public awareness campaigns and government regulation of banquets have persuaded some people to stop consuming the soup. In 2016, it was reported that the consumption of shark fins had fallen in China by more than 80 percent since 2011.[15] However, this was offset by an increase in consumption in Thailand, Vietnam, and Indonesia.

SPORTS

Sports have always been part of Chinese culture. Archery, swordplay, and an ancient form of soccer can all be traced back to the earliest days of the country's recorded history. Some traditional

Lin Dan became a legendary figure in the world of Chinese sports. He went pro in 2001 and retired in 2020 after an incredibly successful career that included two Olympic gold medals.

Chinese sports are still played regionally. Among them is *beikou tarkbei*, a game like field hockey played by the ethnic Daur in Inner Mongolia.

Today, sports such as basketball, soccer, table tennis, cycling, and running are all popular, and Chinese teams frequently dominate in competitive badminton. Two-time Olympic champion and five-time world champion badminton player Lin Dan is from China. With more than 650 career wins, he is one of China's biggest sports idols and is famous throughout Asia.[16] Badminton is widely popular in China as a leisure activity.

Domestically produced hits such as *Operation Red Sea* have made China a key part of the world film industry.

CINEMA

The first Chinese movie, *Dingjun Mountain*, was released in 1905. During the country's civil-war years, Chinese filmmakers used their craft to express their anguish and share it with the people. Between 1949 and 1966, the state took control of the industry, producing hundreds of movies aligned with the party's views. During the Cultural Revolution, the CCP cracked down on filmmakers. The government ordered some to make industrial training films, and it sent others to labor education camps. No commercial movies were made in China between 1966 and 1972.

In 1976, after Mao's death, the government's policies of more openness helped revive the Chinese film industry. In that year, 46 new films were produced and distributed across China. Movies became popular. The government censored movies again for a period in the early 1990s, and only a few low-budget movies were made. In 2000, Taiwanese director Ang Lee produced the most commercially successful Chinese film to date, *Crouching Tiger, Hidden Dragon*. China's film industry has continued to produce blockbusters, such as the 2018 film *Operation Red Sea*, which grossed $579 million globally.[17] Movies again became popular in China. In 2018, China was the second-largest film market in the world, behind only North America. The CCP allows foreign films to be distributed, but the government limits the number of foreign movies that can be imported and censors the ones it allows.

MUSIC

Traditional Chinese music has a history that goes back thousands of years. During the early dynasties, chimes and bells were played for a royal audience. The common people enjoyed singing and dancing at fairs during the Tang dynasty. Opera singers performed in tearooms and theaters during the Song dynasty. There was great regional diversity in opera styles. When the different opera styles were performed together for the royal court, a new style was developed, the

Beijing opera. Chinese peasants also wrote folk songs about daily life and work that were popular among commoners. Traditional Chinese music uses string, percussion, and wind instruments.

The first pop concert performed by a Western artist in China was by the British band Wham! in 1985. Now, many kinds of music are extremely popular in China. Almost three-quarters of the population listen to music every day, enjoying an average of 16 hours of music per week.[18] In the early 2020s, the affluent in China preferred listening to English-language pop, rock, and jazz. Western artists also frequently perform in China now, but there are restrictions. Chinese officials denied rapper Jay-Z from performing because of what they called "vulgar lyrics" in his music. They also prohibited singer Justin Bieber from performing because of his "bad behavior."[19]

There is also a Chinese-language music scene. Chinese popular music, or C-pop, has three major regional subgenres. Cantopop is sung in Cantonese, Mandopop is sung in Mandarin, and Hokkien pop is sung in Taiwanese Hokkien. Chinese artists also work in a wide variety of other musical genres, including rock and hip-hop. Some C-pop groups combine all three languages in their songs to broaden their appeal.

CHINESE OPERA

The first Chinese opera troupe, called the Pear Garden, was founded by Emperor Xuanzong of the Tang dynasty. Today's opera professionals are still called the Disciples of the Pear Garden. Opera was popular among the public and was performed in large public theaters. Different styles of opera flourished in different regions, and the art has evolved over the centuries. There are more than 300 regional styles of opera performed throughout the country.[20]

MINI **BIO**

CONFUCIUS

Confucius was an ancient Chinese philosopher whose teachings have formed the foundation of much of Chinese culture. His teachings were recorded in writings called *Lunyu*, or *The Analects of Confucius*. Confucianism emphasizes a good character, loyalty to oneself, and respect for one's elders. Despite his deep and lengthy influence on Chinese culture, Confucius came from humble beginnings.

There is much debate about his life story because many accounts are considered fictional. *Lunyu* contains the most referenced account of his life. They were not written until after his death, and there is little context in them, so they are not a perfect historical record. He was born in 551 BCE in what is now Shandong province. Confucius's father was a warrior who died shortly after Confucius was born. He grew up fatherless and poor. His aphorisms are still quoted, including his golden rule: "Do not do unto others what you would not want others to do unto you."[21] Confucius died in 479 BCE.

Confucius has had a significant impact on philosophy in China, throughout Asia, and in many other parts of the world.

CHAPTER **SIX**

POLITICS

The CCP has dominated politics in China since the establishment of the PRC in 1949. Since then, the nation has remained a one-party state. The party has spearheaded massive economic reform in the country, lifting hundreds of millions of people out of poverty. At the same time, it sharply curtails the rights of its citizens, heavily censors the media, and engages in massive surveillance to reinforce its power and authority in the country.

China's current constitution was adopted on December 4, 1982. The constitution empowers the National People's Congress (NPC) and the party's Politburo Standing Committee. It also outlines the division of responsibility for provinces, counties, and municipalities. The constitution has been amended several times. The constitution states that the CCP

The National People's Congress meets in the Great Hall of the People in Beijing.

is the country's only political party and that all rights belong to the people. It also guarantees all ethnic groups equality and grants citizens freedom of speech, correspondence, the press, assembly, association, and demonstration. Freedom of religious belief and the right to criticize the government are also among the rights in the constitution. However, these rights are often disregarded in practice. Article 51 of the constitution essentially negates other articles, stating, "When exercising their freedoms and rights, citizens of the People's Republic of China (PRC) shall not undermine the interests of the state."[1]

THE PEOPLE'S LIBERATION ARMY (PLA)

The PLA is the military of China. However, it is not technically a national army but rather the armed forces of a political party, the CCP. Founded in 1927, the PLA includes China's ground, navy, and air forces, as well as the strategic missile corps. It has more than two million active personnel and more than one million reservists, making it the largest standing army in the world.[2] Aside from national defense and military operations, the PLA also oversees antipiracy, emergency response, and disaster-relief efforts. The PLA's primary role is to protect the CCP.

BRANCHES OF GOVERNMENT

The PRC's government is broken into three branches: executive, legislative, and judicial. The executive branch includes the president, who is the head of state, and the vice president. They are both elected by the NPC for a five-year term, with no term limits. In 2022, the president was Xi Jinping. He was first elected in March 2013 and was reelected in March 2018 with 100 percent of the NPC's vote. The executive branch also includes the premier, who is the head of government, and the executive vice premiers. The president nominates the premier, who is then confirmed by the NPC.

The president is also the general secretary of the CCP, and this position grants the most power. The CCP controls every government department, military force, court, and parliamentary meeting, and the general secretary is at the head of it all. The most powerful politicians in China are the seven members of the Politburo Standing Committee. These seven members are part of the wider politburo, which has 18 additional members. The politburo oversees the CCP, making the most important decisions that affect the country.

The NPC is China's legislature. It was designed to write laws and oversee the government. In reality, it answers to the CCP. The congress

In June 2022, Xi Jinping gave a speech commemorating the 25th anniversary of Chinese control over Hong Kong.

includes a maximum of 3,000 members who are elected for five-year terms by municipal, regional, and provincial congresses. However, only CCP party members, approved independent candidates, or members of one of the eight CCP-affiliated parties are ever elected. Citizens aged 18 and older can vote. They vote directly for members of the lowest People's Congress at the county level. Delegates from that congress then elect members for the next level of congress, and so on. These People's Congresses generally have little say or power over government affairs, and the CCP makes most significant decisions.

The judiciary is the third branch of the government. It is made of multiple parts. There is the Supreme People's Court, which is the highest court in the country, as well as lower-level People's Courts and International Commercial Courts. There are also special courts focusing on military, maritime, transportation, and forestry issues. The NPC appoints the Supreme People's Court's chief justice, who is limited to two consecutive five-year terms. The chief justice nominates other judges. The NPC Standing Committee then appoints them and determines their terms. The Supreme

OTHER POLITICAL PARTIES

The Chinese government describes itself as having "multi-party cooperation," but all political parties fall under the leadership of the CCP.[3] They include the Nationalist Party, the China Democratic League, the China National Democratic Construction Association, the China Association for Promoting Democracy, the Chinese Peasants and Workers Democratic Party, the China Zhi Gong Party, the Jiu San Society, and the Taiwan Democratic Self-Government League. Together they form the Chinese People's Political Consultative Conference.

People's Court oversees the lower courts, which resolve disputes and criminal cases. But unlike in the United States, its role does not include interpreting the constitution. Instead, that power is reserved for the Standing Committee.

ADMINISTRATIVE AND AUTONOMOUS REGIONS

The government has divided the country into 34 administrative divisions. These are 23 provinces, four municipalities, five autonomous regions, and two special administrative regions.[4] Taiwan, an island approximately 100 miles (161 km) off the southeast coast of China, declared its independence from mainland China in 1949, but the Chinese government still views it as a province.[5]

The five autonomous regions are Guangxi Zhuangzu, Inner Mongolia, Ningxia Huizu, Xinjiang, and Tibet. Chinese laws give these regions the right to self-govern. However, the people of these regions are sometimes subjected to heavy government surveillance. For example, Uighur Muslims caught praying or Tibetans caught posting online about the Dalai Lama—the spiritual leader and former head of state of Tibet—may go to prison.

Hong Kong and Macao are the two special administrative districts. Hong Kong was once occupied by the British. Macao was once occupied by the Portuguese. China regained rule over Hong Kong on July 1, 1997, and established the Hong Kong Special Administrative Region. It also regained control of Macao on December 20, 1999, and established the Macao Special Administrative Region. The two regions abide by a policy China calls "one country, two systems."

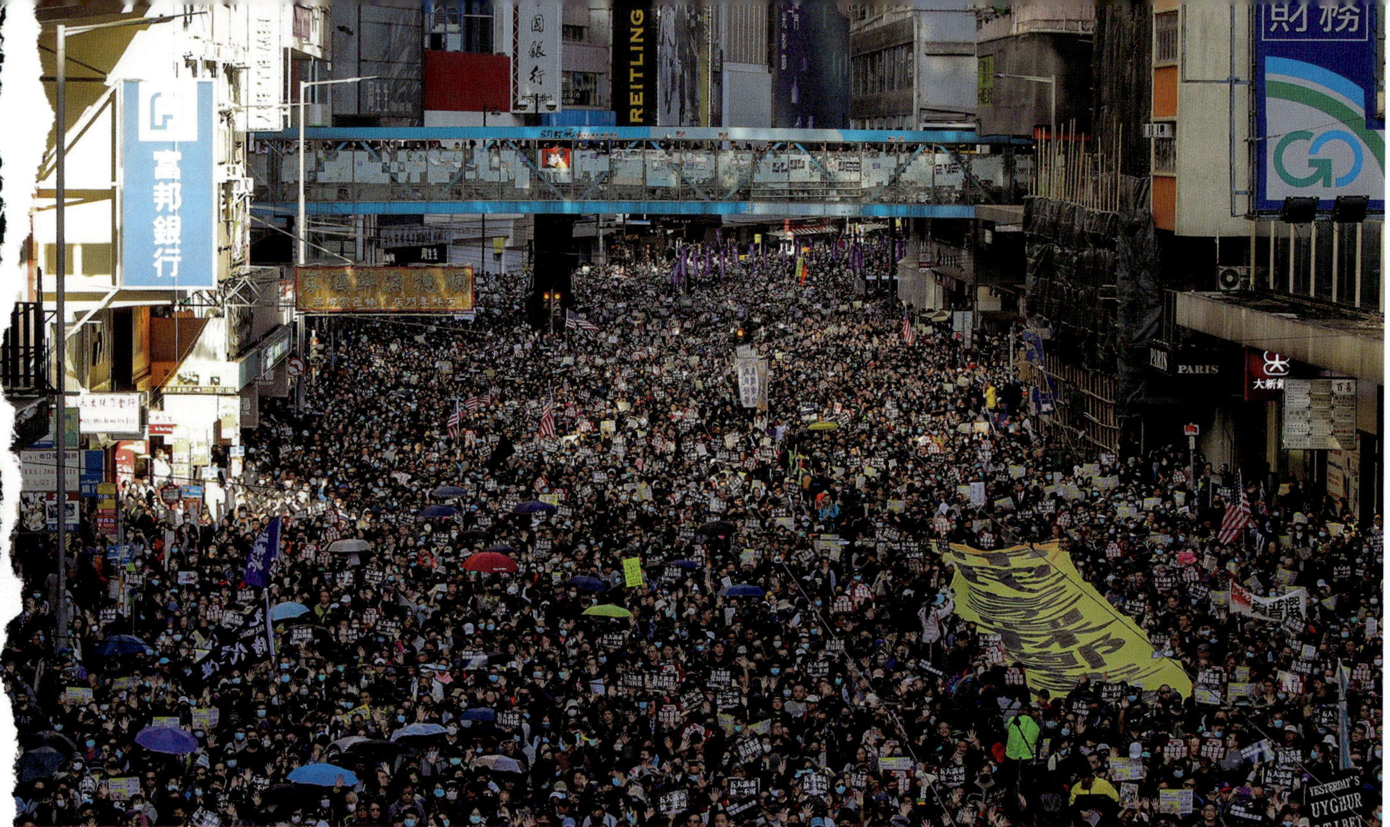

Massive prodemocratic protests broke out in Hong Kong in 2019 after the central Chinese government began imposing more control over the city.

This means that while China is a communist country where the mainland applies a socialist system, the two regions continue to operate under the capitalist system they had been using before they returned to Chinese control.

When Hong Kong returned to Chinese control, the Chinese government promised to give Hong Kong 50 years to maintain its capitalist system and political freedoms. But in 2019, the government started going back on that promise. Over the next few years, it imposed laws restricting freedom of speech and of the press in the name of national security. Government forces began arresting journalists, activists, and lawmakers.

FOREIGN RELATIONS

China is a member of the United Nations (UN) and, along with the other victors of World War II, is one of the five permanent members of the UN Security Council. The country has strong ties with Pakistan, providing the neighbor with weapons and diplomatic support. North Korea is also a longtime ally, and public statements between Xi and North Korean dictator Kim Jong-Un have highlighted their continued partnership. India and China have been involved in border disputes since the end of World War II, a situation that occasionally erupts into isolated pockets of violence. Still, the countries have maintained strong economic ties. The Chinese foreign minister visited India in March 2022, and trade between the two countries increased in the previous year, with Chinese exports to India up 46 percent and Indian exports to China up 34 percent.[5]

Eight US presidents visited China between 1972 and 2022. George W. Bush visited four times, the most of any president.

China and the United States have had a complicated diplomatic relationship. After World War II, the United States sided with the exiled Republic of China government in Taiwan. Then, during the Korean War (1950–1953), the United States and the UN supported South Korea.

US president Richard Nixon, *right*, visited China in 1972, opening a new era in the relationship between the two countries.

PING-PONG DIPLOMACY

An early example of diplomacy between the United States and the PRC came about as a result of table tennis. A pair of US and Chinese table tennis players exchanged gifts on a shuttle bus during the World Table Tennis Championships in Japan in 1971. It was caught on camera. The surprise exchange and sharing of goodwill captured people's attention, and it became the talk of the tournament. Mao used it as a political opportunity, and he invited the US team on an all-expenses-paid trip to China. The players and journalists who joined them were among the first Americans to enter China since the CCP took power in 1949. The media nicknamed this "ping-pong diplomacy."

China sent troops to support communist North Korea. More than 2.5 million civilians and soldiers died before an armistice agreement was signed in 1953.[6]

Between 1954 and 1970, the United States and China were on the opposite sides of several issues. But in 1969, a fraying relationship between the Soviet Union and China opened a door for establishing relations with the United States and other western governments. In 1971, the UN officially gave the PRC the seat that had been held since 1945 by the exiled Republic of China. In 1979, US president Jimmy Carter formalized China's diplomatic relationship with the United States. The United States officially recognized the CCP and severed official relations with Taiwan, though it retained unofficial ties. President Bill Clinton signed the US-China Relations Act of 2000, which granted China normal trade relations with the United States. This was an important development that helped China join the World Trade Organization in 2001. Just a few years later, in 2006, China became the United States' second-biggest trading partner.

CHAPTER **SEVEN**

ECONOMICS

In the first decades after the communist takeover in 1949, the government controlled China's economy. It owned all the businesses and controlled the markets, prices, and production. The nation's economy fared poorly during this period. In the 1960s, China's gross domestic product (GDP) per capita fell behind those of developing nations such as Cambodia and Sierra Leone. In 1976, Mao's successor, Deng Xiaoping, recognized that China was struggling in its economic development. To spur economic growth, he opened trade and lifted price controls, allowing the free market to determine prices. Subsequent leaders also took measures to strengthen China's economy, including allowing private ownership of companies. By 2018, private companies were responsible for half of

Deng Xiaoping set China on a path toward rapid economic development, and he is still widely honored in the country today.

All modern Chinese banknotes include images of Mao Zedong.

China's GDP.[1] These measures led to one of the greatest economic turnarounds in world history.

The nation averaged 10 percent annual growth in the 1980s, 1990s, and early 2000s.[2] In 2022, China's GDP reached $17.46 trillion, making it the second-largest economy in the world behind the United States.[3] Economists predicted it would surpass the United States by 2030. However, its per-capita GDP was $10,434.78 in 2020, a figure that lagged behind many other nations. In that same year, the per-capita GDP of the United States was more than six times greater, at $63,206.50.[4]

The Chinese currency is the renminbi, and its basic unit is the yuan. Other currencies' values fluctuate according to the market, but the yuan's value is set by the government. It pegs the value to a collection of currencies it trades with, always ensuring a favorable exporting exchange rate. In 2022, the yuan was worth about 15 US cents.[5]

LABOR FORCE AND EMPLOYMENT

China's workforce, made up of approximately 776 million people, is the largest in the world.[6] According to the Chinese government, the overall unemployment rate in 2021 was relatively low at 3.96 percent.[7] However, this data may be incomplete, because the Chinese government only tracked employment statistics from urban centers.

In 1958, the CCP introduced a household registration system called *hukou*. Its purpose was to control migration within the country, distribute government welfare and resources, and monitor criminal activity. The hukou system kept people in rural areas working in agriculture, so there was always a steady supply of food for the country.

When the economy took off in the 1980s, more labor was needed in urban centers. This led to what has been described as one of the greatest human migrations of all time. Hundreds of millions of young Chinese people moved from their rural homes to work in the manufacturing and construction industries of the nation's coastal urban areas. Migrant workers have been the backbone of China's economic growth, but they are marginalized and often face institutionalized

HUKOU

In China, every jurisdiction issues its own passport to its citizens. The passport identifies each person's hukou. This document both restricts a person's ability to travel beyond their province and grants that person access to social services within the jurisdiction. The government classifies citizens as rural or urban. The hukou is hereditary. This means that children inherit the hukou classification of their parents regardless of where the children are born and raised.

discrimination. They receive low pay, work many hours, and have few benefits. The country is now facing a potential worker shortage because of an aging population and slow population growth. Between 2010 and 2020, the number of people aged 15 to 59 dropped by 6.79 percent.[8]

Despite the economic policies of the last several decades pulling more than 800 million people out of poverty, China ranked among the worst countries in the world for income inequality in 2020. The combined wealth of the top 1 percent of income earners was greater than that of the bottom 50 percent combined. Housing was also becoming less affordable in cities. The cost of an apartment in the city of Shenzhen was 43.5 times higher than the average income.[9]

In 2021, 292.5 million people migrated to work, a 2.4 percent increase from 2020.[10]

INDUSTRY AND RESOURCES

China is a vast nation with abundant natural resources. These range from fish and water to coal and natural gas. The country has the world's largest deposits of tin, tungsten, and rare earth elements. It mines more gold and iron ore domestically than any other country. With its vast network of rivers and many mountain ranges, it also has the world's largest hydropower potential.

China's three largest sectors are manufacturing, services, and agriculture. It is the largest manufacturer in the world and has become known as the world's factory. Cheap labor, few regulations, low taxes, and favorable foreign currency exchange rates combine to make China

China gets a significant proportion of its electricity from coal. Large groups of workers descend into mines to complete the dangerous work of mining coal.

an attractive place for the world's companies to manufacture goods. Industry, including manufacturing, mining, construction, and utilities, accounted for 39.4 percent of GDP in 2021. The service industry made up 53.3 percent of GDP, and agriculture totaled 7.3 percent of GDP. The figure for agriculture had dropped from 8.94 percent in 2013, but China was still the largest agricultural producer in the world.[11] The country is the world's largest grower of apples, cucumbers, grapes, and rice.

China exports broadcast equipment, computers, steel, textiles, apparel, footwear, toys, electronics, chemicals, fertilizer, and other products to more than 100 countries across the globe. It is the largest exporter in the world, handling approximately 15 percent of global exports.[12] This puts the country's economy at risk should any of its major trading partners decrease the amount they import from China. This has led the CCP to shift its economic policy to focus on the domestic market. The idea is to take advantage of the nation's enormous population and the potential of domestic demand to balance reliance on exports. In 2020, household spending, or money spent by people on everyday needs such as housing, clothing, and food, accounted for only 38 percent of the economy. By comparison, household spending was approximately 60 percent of GDP in the United States, Canada, and the United Kingdom.[13]

The United States is China's largest export partner. China exported about $438 billion worth of goods to the United States in 2020.[14]

INFRASTRUCTURE AND TRANSPORTATION

China's rapid economic development and large number of migrant workers have led to an efficient transportation network. Most people and cargo travel by road. From 2010 to 2020, the country's network of freeways almost doubled in size.[15] In 2020, approximately 37 million short tons (34 million metric tons) of freight traveled on China's roads.[16] The rapid growth of roadways has led to traffic congestion problems in some cities.

China also has an extensive passenger and freight rail system. In 2020, China had 87,900 miles (141,400 km) of operating rail lines. In the year before that, 3.66 billion passengers traveled by rail.[17] The amount of cargo transported by train in 2020 was 3.95 billion short tons (3.58 billion metric tons).[18] China's bodies of water are also an important form of transportation for both people and cargo. The country is home to seven of the world's ten largest seaports. The Yangtze River is the primary inland waterway and, at about 3,915 miles (6,300 km) long, is also the country's longest.[19]

Buses are a key mode of public transportation within and between cities, carrying approximately 70 billion passengers a year. China has also built extensive subway systems, operating 275 lines

PORT OF SHANGHAI

The Chinese started developing the Port of Shanghai during the Ming dynasty. It became a significant seaport after 1684, when the Qing dynasty allowed the port to accept oceangoing vessels. Located at the mouth of the Yangtze River, it has both a river port and deep seaport. Today, the port is the largest in the world in terms of shipment tonnage.

In 2010, a traffic jam on the Beijing-Tibet Expressway was 62 miles (100 km) long.[23]

covering 5,428 miles (8,736 km) in 2021. Taxis are another popular mode of transportation. In 2021, there were roughly 1.4 million taxis in the cities, and they transported approximately 27 million passengers.[20]

TOURISM

The tourism industry in China experienced substantial growth in the first few decades of the 2000s. In 2019, the industry generated $986 billion in revenue, and it created jobs for nearly 80 million people.[21] The largest share of foreign travelers come from South Korea, with the country receiving more than four million South Korean visitors in 2018. Japan, Russia, and the United States were the next largest sources of tourists, with approximately 2.5 million visitors from each country in 2018.[22]

However, the COVID-19 pandemic brought extensive and long-lasting travel restrictions. In 2019, domestic travelers took six billion domestic trips. The three most popular destinations for domestic travelers were Xinjiang, Beijing, and Taiwan. The number of domestic travelers fell as the pandemic continued. Revenue from travel and tourism dropped sharply, and with international travel still difficult or impossible, almost all tourists in 2021 were domestic.

Each year, millions of tourists from China and around the world visit the accessible segments of the Great Wall.

CHAPTER **EIGHT**

CHINA TODAY

China in 2022 was a far different country than it was just a handful of decades earlier. It shifted from being one of the poorest nations in the world to the second-largest economy on Earth. The population was more educated, with almost 97 percent of the people literate in 2022 as compared to only 65.5 percent in 1982.[1] With its abundance of both human and natural resources, China is on track to overtake the United States as the world's largest economy. It also has the potential to have a major influence on geopolitical issues such as international trade, climate change, and global conflicts.

But as the economy grows and living standards rise, Chinese citizens are also seeing increased restrictions. The CCP government has taken advantage of technology to broaden its control over the people.

China's sustained growth has ensured that it will remain a powerful and influential player on the world stage in the decades to come.

Surveillance of the population has increased, with video cameras and facial recognition software common in public places. The autonomy of regions such as Hong Kong and Macao has eroded as the CCP works to bring them under its control. The government has persecuted ethnic and religious minorities, such as the Uighurs. And citizens who speak out about the government risk severe consequences. Because the state controls the media and restricts and censors the internet, citizens rarely hear negative things about their government.

A SURVEILLANCE STATE

In 2018, the Chinese government announced its initiative Project Sharp Eyes, which aimed to install video cameras in all of the country's public spaces. The surveillance is used as part of a social credit system in which the government punishes unacceptable behavior such as jaywalking while rewarding positive behavior, such as having a good financial credit rating. If the government assesses people's behavior as good, it gives them access to better schools, the right to travel, or the opportunity to live in a nicer city.

FAMILY STRUCTURE

The family unit is the central structure of Chinese society. Each family member has a clearly defined role. The husband or father is usually the head of the household. He is expected to protect his family, and he expects his wife and children to show respect and obedience.

The influence of Western cultures, along with the separation of families because of their jobs, has meant that these roles are not as strictly followed as they once were. Still, children are expected to obey and honor their elders. Family members consult elders on big decisions, and

Migrant workers attended a job fair in Taizhou in 2021. The increased number of migrant workers has disrupted traditional Chinese family structures.

children care for their parents as they age. It is common for several generations to live in a single household. Family structures have changed with the migration of people from rural areas to urban centers. Many young people now work in the city and send part of their income back to their families. Often their parents pressure them to get married and return to their small hometowns to raise the next generation of the family. But opportunities for prosperity are often found in the cities, so many families remain separated.

In 2021, Chinese households owned 190 million pets, of which 59.5 percent were cats.[2]

EDUCATION AND OPPORTUNITIES

In 1986, the Chinese government passed a compulsory education law that required all children to receive nine years of education. Twelve years later, it began to expand university enrollment. However, earning a place in one of the country's top universities is competitive. Students must take the *gaokao*, a test that determines which university they will be able to attend. Families place a lot of importance on the exam, as getting into a good school may affect the future prosperity of the family.

The hukou system prevents rural students from pursuing an education outside of their home province, and the educational opportunities are not as good in rural areas as they are in the big cities. This means rural children are often at a disadvantage before they even begin studying

Students at a high school in Nanjing watched a presentation given by the three Chinese astronauts aboard the space station Tiangong in late 2021.

for the gaokao. In 2015, it was reported that children from rural areas were 14 times less likely to attend an elite university than their urban counterparts. Almost 80 percent of children younger than 14 had a rural hukou designation, but less than 17 percent of students at elite schools were from rural hukou. It is estimated that 75 percent of urban students attend university, compared to only 15 percent of rural ones.[3] Overseas study has also become a popular choice for students whose parents can afford tuition.

CURRENT CHALLENGES

China has seen incredible growth in the first few decades of the 2000s, but it has also faced critical challenges. Perhaps the largest was the COVID-19 pandemic. This disease was first identified in Wuhan, China, in late 2019. In early 2020, it began to spread around the world and was officially declared a pandemic. In the early weeks of the outbreak, the government worked to suppress news of the spreading disease. Dr. Li Wenliang, the first doctor in China to report a suspected a virus outbreak, was investigated by the Chinese government and told to stop making false comments. He died from COVID-19 on February 7, 2020. Li's death led to public anger toward the government for its handling of the situation.

Once the Chinese government acknowledged COVID-19, it stepped up to produce and export personal protective equipment, ventilators, and other medical supplies around the world. When Chinese scientists developed a vaccine, the country donated millions of doses internationally. However, global demand fell for China's vaccines as they proved less effective than their American- and European-made counterparts.

As with other nations affected by the pandemic, China's economy took a significant hit. Whole cities were locked down to contain the spread of the virus, closing and disrupting businesses

Chinese authorities physically locked down neighborhoods in Shanghai following a COVID-19 outbreak there in 2022. This strategy limited the disease's spread, but it also negatively impacted the economy.

The announcement of a partnership between China and Russia under Vladimir Putin, *left*, suggested that China would not work against Russia's war on Ukraine.

and schools. In 2020, the country had its lowest rate of economic growth in decades, at only 2.2 percent. However, it was the only country to experience any growth in 2020, and by 2021, its annual growth had rebounded to 8.1 percent.[4] By June 2022, the country had reported more than two million cases and more than 14,000 deaths.[5] By comparison, the United States had 86 million confirmed cases and one million deaths.[6]

The pandemic did not distract the Chinese government from political matters. In early February 2022, China signed a significant pact with Russia. In it, the two countries stated there were no "forbidden areas of cooperation." They pledged to "stand shoulder to shoulder against America and the West, ideologically as well as militarily."[7] A few weeks later, Russia invaded Ukraine. Many nations condemned the unprovoked attack, but President Xi Jinping said his country was neutral in the matter and called for a peaceful resolution. The UN General Assembly adopted a resolution to suspend Russia from the Human Rights Council on April 7, 2022. China abstained from the vote.

On May 1, 2022, Ukraine's foreign minister called on the Chinese government to act as a mediator between Ukraine and Russia to help bring the conflict to an end. "China is willing to continue playing a constructive role in urging peace talks and is willing when necessary to work together with the international community to launch required mediation," Foreign Minister Wang Yi told reporters at a news conference.[8]

At home, the Chinese government enacted institutional discrimination against the LGBTQ community. In 2021, its television regulators banned all broadcasters from airing men perceived as effeminate on television. Dozens of LGBTQ websites and social media accounts were shut down.

Because of its rapid development, China has had a poor track record in terms of climate matters. Deforestation, pollution, and hunting have all damaged the country's ecosystems. So has a tremendous increase in urbanization and the number of cars on the nation's roads. Climate change will threaten the country with rising sea levels, more extreme heat waves, and more intense storms. The Chinese government committed to

THE UIGHURS

An issue that frequently attracts international attention in China is the government's treatment of the Uighurs. The Uighurs are a minority ethnic group who are mostly Muslim and speak primarily their own language that is similar to Turkish. They live in the Xinjiang region in northwest China. In the late 2010s and early 2020s, the international community accused the Chinese government of crimes against humanity and even genocide of the Uighurs. The Chinese government has targeted this population with intrusive surveillance, including by having government officials move into homes to monitor people and report behavior to Beijing. In 2014, the government started moving the Uighurs into reeducation camps that news sources have described as labor camps. More than one million Uighurs have been corralled, detained, and forced to work in factories. They work many hours in brutal conditions with no breaks. They take lessons in Mandarin and the party's ideology. There have also been reports of torture and forced sterilization of women.

THE BELT AND ROAD INITIATIVE

In 2013, President Xi Jinping announced a development initiative aimed at significantly increasing China's international power and influence. Known as the Belt and Road Initiative, it involved massive infrastructure construction, including railways, energy pipelines, and highways in Asia, Europe, and Africa. The goal was to boost the world's economic links to China. By 2022, dozens of nations had either signed on to the project or expressed an interest in doing so.

reducing its greenhouse gas emissions under the Paris Agreement, but some critics contend that China's development plans could increase emissions, not decrease them.

China has solidified its status as a world leader. Its long, complex history has influenced cultures and commerce across the globe. It has become immensely powerful, fallen to division and occupation, and risen again many times over the centuries. China's unprecedented economic growth has made it the most important emerging superpower. In the same way that historians have called the 1900s the "American century," some experts in international relations have suggested that the 2000s will become the "Chinese century."[9]

ESSENTIAL **FACTS**

OFFICIAL NAME: PEOPLE'S REPUBLIC OF CHINA

GEOGRAPHY

Area: 3,705,407 square miles (9,596,960 sq km)

Highest Elevation: Mount Everest at 29,032 feet (8,849 m)

Lowest Elevation: The Turfan Depression at –508 feet (–155 m)

PEOPLE

Population: 1.41 billion (2022 est.)

Most Populous City: Shanghai (28.5 million)

Ethnic Groups: Mostly Han Chinese; also ethnic minorities, including Zhang, Hui, Manchu, Uighur, Miao, Yi, Tujia, Tibetan, Mongol, Dong, Buyei, Yao, Bai, Korean, Hani, Li, Kazakh, Dai, others

Religions: Folk religion, Buddhism, Christianity, Islam, Hinduism, Judaism, other, and unaffiliated

GOVERNMENT

Type of Government: Communist Party–led state

Capital: Beijing

Head of State: President

Head of Government: Premier

Legislature: Unicameral, with the National People's Congress

ECONOMY

Currency: Renminbi

Major Industries: Mining, manufacturing consumer goods, textile production, food processing, manufacturing cars, airplanes, and ships

Natural Resources: Coal, iron ore, petroleum, natural gas, metals, rare earth elements, hydropower

NATIONAL SYMBOLS

National Anthem: "Yiyongjun Jinxingqu" ("The March of the Volunteers")

National Bird: Red-crowned crane

National Flower: Plum blossom

GLOSSARY

ANIMISM
A belief that plants, inanimate objects, and places have a spiritual essence.

APHORISM
A concise observation that states a general or obvious truth.

ARABLE
Good for growing crops.

ARID
Land that is too dry to support vegetation.

BOREAL
Of a northern geographical region.

BUREAUCRATIC
Relating to the administrative work of managing an agency through processes that are usually viewed as complex and impersonal.

DELTA
The place where a river empties into a sea.

GROSS DOMESTIC PRODUCT (GDP)

The monetary value of all final goods and services produced within a nation's geographic borders over a specified period of time.

MARITIME

Having to do with the sea or waterways.

MARTIAL LAW

The replacement of civilian rule with military control.

MONSOON

A seasonal wind in South and Southeast Asia between May and September that brings heavy rain.

POLITBURO

A decision-making committee inside a communist party.

SUBSISTENCE

Surviving at the minimum level possible.

ADDITIONAL **RESOURCES**

SELECTED BIBLIOGRAPHY

"China." *CIA World Factbook*, 26 July 2022, cia.gov. Accessed 17 June 2022.

Twitchett, Denis C. "China." *Encyclopedia Britannica*, 14 June 2022, britannica.com. Accessed 17 June 2022.

"U.S. Relations with China." *Council on Foreign Relations*, 2022, cfr.org. Accessed 17 June 2022.

FURTHER READINGS

Allen, John. *Cause and Effect: Ancient China*. ReferencePoint, 2018.

Allen, John. *Growing Up in China*. ReferencePoint, 2018.

Hamen, Susan E. *Fighting COVID-19 Abroad*. Abdo, 2023.

ONLINE RESOURCES

Booklinks NONFICTION NETWORK FREE! ONLINE NONFICTION RESOURCES

To learn more about China, please visit **abdobooklinks.com** or scan this QR code. These links are routinely monitored and updated to provide the most current information available.

MORE INFORMATION

For more information on this subject, contact or visit the following organizations:

Mutianyu Great Wall
CHM7+3JC, Mutianyu Rd.
Huairou District, Beijing, China, 101406
mutianyugreatwall.com
Located about 43 miles (70 km) northeast of the center of Beijing, the Mutianyu section of the Great Wall was designated a tourist viewing location in 2000. Visitors can walk along the wall and learn about its history.

The Palace Museum
4 Jingshan Front St.
Dongcheng, Beijing, China, 100009
en.dpm.org.cn
The Palace Museum is located in the Forbidden City at the center of Beijing. The sprawling museum features a vast assortment of historic art and artifacts.

US Embassy in China
No. 55 An Jia Lou Lu
Beijing, China, 100600
china.usembassy-china.org.cn
The US Embassy in China provides all kinds of services for US citizens, including safety, travel, and cultural information.

SOURCE **NOTES**

CHAPTER 1. A TOUR OF CHINA

1. Marianna Cerini. "Inside Daxing, Beijing's Massive New International Airport." *Condé Nast Traveler*, 29 Oct. 2019, cntraveler.com. Accessed 2 Aug. 2022.
2. "Forbidden City." *Lonely Planet*, n.d., lonelyplanet.com. Accessed 2 Aug. 2022.
3. "Tiananmen Square." *Encyclopedia Britannica*, 15 May 2022, britannica.com. Accessed 2 Aug. 2022.
4. "Why Is the Palace Called the Forbidden City?" *Google Arts and Culture*, n.d., artsandculture.google.com. Accessed 2 Aug. 2022.
5. "Beijing-Shanghai High-Speed Line." *Railway Technology*, 25 July 2000, railway-technology.com. Accessed 2 Aug. 2022.
6. "Tiananmen Square Incident." *Encyclopedia Britannica*, 20 Apr. 2022, britannica.com. Accessed 2 Aug. 2022.

CHAPTER 2. GEOGRAPHY

1. "China." *CIA World Factbook*, 26 July 2022, cia.gov. Accessed 2 Aug. 2022.
2. "China–Mongolia Border." *Google Arts and Culture*, n.d., artsandculture.google.com. Accessed 10 Aug. 2022.
3. Caitlin Dempsey. "Largest Plateau in the World." *Geography Realm*, 27 Jan. 2022, geographyrealm.com. Accessed 2 Aug. 2022.
4. Vasily Mikhaylovich Sinitsyn. "Kunlun Mountains." *Encyclopedia Britannica*, 29 Dec. 2019, britannica.com. Accessed 10 Aug. 2022.
5. Amar Toor. "Why Did 28,000 Rivers in China Suddenly Disappear?" *Verge*, 3 Apr. 2013, theverge.com. Accessed 2 Aug. 2022.
6. "Rivers and Lakes in China." *China.org.cn*, n.d., china.org.cn. Accessed 2 Aug. 2022.
7. "Save Our Earth's Kidney." *China through a Lens*, 1 July 2002, china.org.cn. Accessed 10 Aug. 2022.
8. "Yarlung Tsangpo: The Everest of Rivers." *NASA Earth Observatory*, 25 Feb. 2001, earthobservatory.nasa.gov. Accessed 2 Aug. 2022.
9. Stephen Venables. "Mount Everest." *Encyclopedia Britannica*, 12 May 2022, britannica.com. Accessed 2 Aug. 2022.
10. Daniel Rechtschaffen. "How China's Growing Deserts Are Choking the Country." *Forbes*, 18 Sept. 2017, forbes.com. Accessed 2 Aug. 2022.
11. "China," *CIA World Factbook*.
12. Aleksandr Pavlovich Muranov. "Yangtze River." *Encyclopedia Britannica*, 3 Feb. 2022, britannica.com. Accessed 2 Aug. 2022.
13. "Cultural Landscape of Honghe Hani Rice Terraces." *UNESCO*, n.d., whc.unesco.org. Accessed 2 Aug. 2022.
14. "Climate of China." *Consulate-General of the People's Republic of China in Gothenburg*, n.d., fmprc.gov.cn. Accessed 2 Aug. 2022.
15. Kelly Pang. "10 Facts to Familiarize Yourself with China's Weather Ahead of Your Trip." *China Highlights*, 4 Jan. 2022, chinahighlights.com. Accessed 2 Aug. 2022.
16. "Climate of China," *Consulate-General of the People's Republic of China in Gothenburg*.
17. "Mount Huangshan." *UNESCO*, n.d., whc.unesco.org. Accessed 2 Aug. 2022.

CHAPTER 3. PLANTS AND ANIMALS

1. Li You. "The Biggest Winners from China's Protected Species List? Wolves." *Sixth Tone*, 19 Feb. 2021, sixthtone.com. Accessed 2 Aug. 2022.
2. Rhett A. Butler. "Countries with the Highest Biodiversity." *Mongabay*, 1 July 2019, rainforests.mongabay.com. Accessed 2 Aug. 2022.
3. Kyle Obermann. "China Declares Pandas No Longer Endangered—but Threats Persist." *National Geographic*, 1 Sept. 2021, nationalgeographic.com. Accessed 2 Aug. 2022.
4. "Wild Pandas Get a Boost." *World Wildlife Fund*, Spring 2017, worldwildlife.org. Accessed 2 Aug. 2022.
5. "Wild Pandas Get a Boost," *World Wildlife Fund*.

6. Kyle Obermann, "China Declares Pandas No Longer Endangered—but Threats Persist."
7. "Chinese Alligator." *WCS China*, n.d., china.wcs.org. Accessed 2 Aug. 2022.
8. Erik Stokstad. "China Moves to Protect Coastal Wetlands Used by Migratory Birds." *Science*, 30 Jan. 2018, science.org. Accessed 2 Aug. 2022.
9. Dale Hoiberg. "Traditional Chinese Medicine and Endangered Animals." *Encyclopedia Britannica*, 22 Oct. 2007, britannica.com. Accessed 2 Aug. 2022.
10. Tin Lok Wu. "Chinese Deforestation and Lessons from Its Conservation Efforts." *Earth.org*, 14 Feb. 2022, earth.org. Accessed 2 Aug. 2022.
11. "How China Brought Its Forests Back to Life in a Decade." *Rapid Transition Alliance*, 2 Dec. 2018, rapidtransition.org. Accessed 2 Aug. 2022.
12. "Xishuangbanna Biosphere Reserve, China." *UNESCO*, n.d., en.unesco.org. Accessed 2 Aug. 2022.
13. "Biosphere Reserves." *UNESCO*, n.d., en.unesco.org. Accessed 2 Aug. 2022.
14. Keith Bradsher. "China's Concrete Jungles Make Room for Green Space." *New York Times*, 1 June 2021, nytimes.com. Accessed 2 Aug. 2022.
15. Matthew Keyte. "10 Beautiful National Parks in China." *Culture Trip*, 9 Feb. 2017, theculturetrip.com. Accessed 2 Aug. 2022.
16. Keyte, "10 Beautiful National Parks in China."
17. Keyte, "10 Beautiful National Parks in China."
18. "Nature Reserves." *China.org.cn*, n.d., china.org.cn. Accessed 2 Aug. 2022.

CHAPTER 4. HISTORY

1. Scott Smith. "Top 10 Facts about the Terracotta Warriors." *National Museums Liverpool*, 2022, liverpoolmuseums.org.uk. Accessed 2 Aug. 2022.
2. Li Yang and Huo Yan. "An Ancient Thoroughfare Sleeps below the Soil." *China Daily*, 2 May 2019, chinadaily.com.cn. Accessed 2 Aug. 2022.
3. Melanie Lieberman. "17 Secrets of the Great Wall of China." *Travel + Leisure*, 20 Apr. 2017, travelandleisure.com. Accessed 2 Aug. 2022.
4. Mark Cartwright. "Song Dynasty." *World History Encyclopedia*, 26 Sept. 2017, worldhistory.org. Accessed 2 Aug. 2022.
5. "Qing Dynasty." *Encyclopedia Britannica*, 10 Apr. 2022, britannica.com. Accessed 2 Aug. 2022.
6. Abby Rogers. "The 10 Greatest Empires in the History of the World." *Insider*, 9 Nov. 2011, businessinsider.com. Accessed 2 Aug. 2022.
7. "Boxer Rebellion." *Encyclopedia Britannica*, 13 Feb. 2020, britannica.com. Accessed 2 Aug. 2022.
8. Lorraine Boissoneault. "The Surprisingly Important Role China Played in WWI." *Smithsonian Magazine*, 17 Aug. 2017, smithsonianmag.com. Accessed 2 Aug. 2022.
9. Shujie Yao. "Economic Development and Poverty Reduction in China over 20 Years of Reforms." *Economic Development and Cultural Change*, Apr. 2000, journals.uchicago.edu. Accessed 2 Aug. 2022.
10. "Great Leap Forward." *Encyclopedia Britannica*, 18 Feb. 2020, britannica.com. Accessed 2 Aug. 2022.
11. Tom Phillips. "The Cultural Revolution: All You Need to Know about China's Political Convulsion." *Guardian*, 10 May 2016, theguardian.com. Accessed 2 Aug. 2022.

CHAPTER 5. PEOPLE AND CULTURE

1. "China." *CIA World Factbook*, 26 July 2022, cia.gov. Accessed 2 Aug. 2022.
2. "2022 Population by Country." *World Population Review*, 2022, worldpopulationreview.com. Accessed 2 Aug. 2022.

SOURCE **NOTES** CONTINUED

3. Andrew Mullen. "China's One-Child Policy: What Was It and What Impact Did It Have?" *China Macro Economy*, 1 June 2021, scmp.com. Accessed 2 Aug. 2022.
4. Carl Minzner. "China's Doomed Fight against Demographic Decline." *Foreign Affairs*, 3 May 2022, foreignaffairs.com. Accessed 2 Aug. 2022.
5. "China's Rapid Urbanization: Benefits, Challenges & Strategies." *World Bank*, 19 June 2008, worldbank.org. Accessed 2 Aug. 2022.
6. "Population of Cities in China (2022)." *World Population Review*, 2022, worldpopulationreview.com. Accessed 2 Aug. 2022.
7. "Beijing Says 400 Million Chinese Cannot Speak Mandarin." *BBC News*, 6 Sept. 2013, bbc.com. Accessed 2 Aug. 2022.
8. "China," *CIA World Factbook*.
9. "China," *CIA World Factbook*.
10. "China," *CIA World Factbook*.
11. Eleanor Albert. "Christianity in China." *Council on Foreign Relations*, 11 Oct. 2018, cfr.org. Accessed 2 Aug. 2022.
12. Crystal Wong. "Record for World's Most Expensive Ceramic, Chinese Imperial Revolving Vase Fetches US$41.6m at Beijing Auction." *Value*, 10 June 2021, en.thevalue.com. Accessed 2 Aug. 2022.
13. "Beijing National Stadium." *Design Build Network*, 20 Jan. 2020, designbuild-network.com. Accessed 2 Aug. 2022.
14. "Beijing National Stadium," *Design Build Network*.
15. Simon Denyer. "Even as China Turns Away from Shark Fin Soup, the Prestige Dish Is Gaining Popularity Elsewhere in Asia." *Washington Post*, 15 Feb. 2018, washingtonpost.com. Accessed 2 Aug. 2022.
16. Jonathan Selvaraj. "'Lin Dan Is Undoubtedly the Greatest. He Is Alone at the Top.'" *ESPN*, 4 July 2020, espn.com. Accessed 2 Aug. 2022.
17. "History." *Economic Cinema*, 2019, economiccinema.com. Accessed 2 Aug. 2022.
18. Mark Savage. "China's Music Listening Habits Revealed." *BBC News*, 2 Feb. 2016, bbc.com. Accessed 2 Aug. 2022.
19. Tom Phillips. "Justin Bieber Banned from China for 'Bad Behaviour.'" *Guardian*, 21 July 2017, theguardian.com. Accessed 2 Aug. 2022.
20. Ronan O'Connell. "The Players of Beijing: How the Peking Opera Is Still Capturing Audiences 200 Years On." *National*, 11 Dec. 2019, thenationalnews.com. Accessed 2 Aug. 2022.
21. "Confucianism." *National Geographic*, 20 May 2022, education.nationalgeographic.org. Accessed 2 Aug. 2022.

CHAPTER 6. POLITICS

1. James A. Dorn. "China's Constitutional Rights: A Grand Illusion." *Cato Institute*, 1 Sept. 2021, cato.org. Accessed 2 Aug. 2022.
2. "Largest Armies in the World Ranked by Active Military Personnel in 2022." *Statista*, 2022, statista.com. Accessed 2 Aug. 2022.
3. "Democratic Parties." *Embassy of the People's Republic of China in the Republic of Liberia*, n.d., mfa.gov.cn. Accessed 2 Aug. 2022.
4. "China." *CIA World Factbook*, 26 July 2022, cia.gov. Accessed 2 Aug. 2022.
5. John C. Copper. "Taiwan." *Encyclopedia Britannica*, 7 Aug. 2022, britannica.com. Accessed 10 Aug. 2022.
6. Meghna Srivastava and Yves Tiberghien. "The Paradox of China-India Relations." *East Asia Forum*, 26 Mar. 2022, eastasiaforum.org. Accessed 2 Aug. 2022.
7. Allan R. Millett. "Korean War." *Encyclopedia Britannica*, 18 June 2022, britannica.com. Accessed 2 Aug. 2022.

CHAPTER 7. ECONOMICS

1. "China's Economy." *Asialink Business*, n.d., asialinkbusiness.com.au. Accessed 2 Aug. 2022.
2. "China GDP – Gross Domestic Product." *Country Economy*, 2022, countryeconomy.com. Accessed 2 Aug. 2022.
3. Caleb Silver. "The Top 25 Economies in the World." *Investopedia*, 27 June 2022, investopedia.com. Accessed 2 Aug. 2022.

4. "GDP Per Capita (Current US$) – China." *World Bank*, 2021, data.worldbank.org. Accessed 2 Aug. 2022.

5. "Convert Chinese Yuan Renminbi to US Dollars." *XE*, 2022, xe.com. Accessed 10 Aug. 2022.

6. "Labor Force – Country Rankings." *Global Economy*, 2021, theglobaleconomy.com. Accessed 2 Aug. 2022.

7. "Registered Unemployment Rate in Urban China from 2010 to 2020." *Statista*, 27 July 2022, statista.com. Accessed 2 Aug. 2022.

8. Andrew Mullen. "China Jobs: Workforce, Unemployment and Retirement Age Explained." *China Macro Economy*, 26 July 2021, scmp.com. Accessed 2 Aug. 2022.

9. Sharon Chen. "China Has a Huge Wealth-Gap Problem." *Bloomberg*, 24 Dec. 2020, bloomberg.com. Accessed 2 Aug. 2022.

10. "Migrant Workers and Their Children." *China Labour Bulletin*, 26 May 2022, clb.org.hk. Accessed 2 Aug. 2022.

11. Prableen Bajpai. "China's GDP Examined." *Investopedia*, 18 Apr. 2022, investopedia.com. Accessed 2 Aug. 2022.

12. David Uren. "Fact: China's Economy Remains Dependent on Exports." *National Interest*, 13 Sept. 2020, nationalinterest.org. Accessed 2 Aug. 2022.

13. "Household Spending." *OECD*, 2022, data.oecd.org. Accessed 2 Aug. 2022.

14. "China." *OECD*, n.d., oec.world. Accessed 2 Aug. 2022.

15. "Transport Infrastructure in China – Statistics & Facts." *Statista*, 20 Apr. 2022, statista.com. Accessed 2 Aug. 2022.

16. "Cargo Volume in Road Freight Traffic in China from 2008 to 2021." *Statista*, 10 June 2022, statista.com. Accessed 2 Aug. 2022.

17. Wang Keju. "Rail Network Gets Boost; More Tracks to Be High Speed." *China Daily*, 13 Aug. 2020, chinadaily.com.cn. Accessed 10 Aug. 2022.

18. "China Rail Freight Volume Up 3.1 Pct in 2020." *Xinhua*, 6 Mar. 2021, xinhuanet.com. Accessed 2 Aug. 2022.

19. Aleksandr Pavlovich Muranov. "Yangtze River." *Encyclopedia Britannica*, 3 Feb. 2022, britannica.com. Accessed 2 Aug. 2022.

20. "Transport Infrastructure in China – Statistics & Facts," *Statista*.

21. Agne Blazyte. "Number of Employees in the Travel and Tourism Industry in China from 2016 to 2019, by Type." *Statista*, 6 July 2022, statista.com. Accessed 2 Aug. 2022.

22. "Countries of Origin of Foreign Tourists in China in 2018." *Statista*, 23 June 2022, statista.com. Accessed 2 Aug. 2022.

23. Jim Gorzelany. "The Worst Traffic Jams in History." *Forbes*, 21 May 2013, forbes.com. Accessed 2 Aug. 2022.

CHAPTER 8. CHINA TODAY

1. "Adult Literacy Rate in China from 1982 to 2018." *Statista*, 27 July 2022, statista.com. Accessed 2 Aug. 2022.

2. Yihan Ma. "Most Popular Pets in Urban Households in China from 2019 to 2021, by Pet Type." *Statista*, 16 Feb. 2022, statista.com. Accessed 2 Aug. 2022.

3. "Education in China Is Becoming Increasingly Unfair to the Poor." *Economist*, 27 May 2021, economist.com. Accessed 2 Aug. 2022.

4. "COVID-19 Brief: Impact on China's Global Influence." *US Global Leadership Coalition*, n.d., usglc.org. Accessed 2 Aug. 2022.

5. Wenyi Zhang. "Number of Novel Coronavirus COVID-19 Cumulative Confirmed and Death Cases in China from January 20, 2020 to June 6, 2022." *Statista*, 27 July 2022, statista.com. Accessed 2 Aug. 2022.

6. John Elflein. "Total Number of Cases and Deaths from Coronavirus (COVID-19) in the United States as of July 22, 2022." *Statista*, 27 July 2022, statista.com. Accessed 2 Aug. 2022.

7. Robin Wright. "Russia and China Unveil a Pact against America and the West." *New Yorker*, 7 Feb. 2022, newyorker.com. Accessed 2 Aug. 2022.

8. Christian Shepherd. "China Touts 'Rock Solid' Ties with Russia as It Offers to Mediate Ukraine Conflict." *Washington Post*, 7 Mar. 2022, washingtonpost.com. Accessed 2 Aug. 2022.

9. "The Chinese Century Is Well Under Way." *Economist*, 27 Oct. 2018, economist.com. Accessed 2 Aug. 2022.

INDEX

ABOUT THE **AUTHOR**

RACQUEL FORAN

Racquel Foran is a freelance writer from Coquitlam, British Columbia, Canada. She has authored several nonfiction titles for school-age readers covering diverse subjects, such as organ transplants, autism spectrum disorder, and North Korea, among others. When she is not writing, she enjoys tending to her Little Free Library, painting, and walking her dogs by the river.